My Decade at Old Sun,
My Lifetime of Hell

My Decade at Old Sun, My Lifetime of Hell

ARTHUR BEAR CHIEF

AU PRESS

"My Decade at Old Sun, My Lifetime of Hell" © 2016 Arthur Bear Chief
Preface © 2016 Judy Bedford
Afterword © 2016 Frits Pannekoek

Published by AU Press, Athabasca University
1200, 10011 – 109 Street, Edmonton, Alberta T5J 3S8

ISBN 978-1-77199-175-9 (pbk.)   ISBN 978-1-77199-176-6 (pdf)
ISBN 978-1-77199-177-3 (epub)   DOI: 10.15215/aupress/9781771991759.01

Cover design by design by Marvin Harder, marvinharder.com
Interior design by Sergiy Kozakov
Printed and bound in Canada by Marquis Book Printers

Library and Archives Canada Cataloguing in Publication

Bear Chief, Arthur, 1942–, author

My decade at Old Sun, my lifetime of hell / Arthur Bear Chief.

(Our lives: diary, memoir, and letters)
Issued in print and electronic formats.

1. Bear Chief, Arthur, 1942–. 2. Abused Indian students—Alberta—
Gleichen—Biography. 3. Adult child abuse victims—Alberta—Gleichen—
Biography. 4. Siksika Indians—Alberta—Biography. 5. Indians of North
America—Alberta—Residential Schools. 6. Old Sun Indian Residential
School (Gleichen, Alta.). 7. Siksika Indians—Education—Alberta. 8.
Gleichen (Alta.). 9. Siksika Indians—Social life and customs. I. Title. II.
Series: Our lives (Edmonton, Alta.)

E99.S54B43 2016   371.829'97352   C2016-906831-5

                                              C2016-906832-3

We acknowledge the financial support of the Government of Canada
through the Canada Book Fund (CBF) for our publishing activities and the
Canada Council for the Arts, which last year invested $153 million to bring
the arts to Canadians throughout the country.

Assistance provided by the Government of Alberta, Alberta Media Fund.

 Canada Council
for the Arts

Conseil des Arts
du Canada

 Canadian
Heritage

Patrimoine
canadien

 Alberta
Government

This book is dedicated to members of the Siksika community, many of them now deceased, who attended Old Sun Indian Residential School. May we who survive purge ourselves of our demons and move forward together.

ARTHUR BEAR CHIEF

SIKSIKA, ALBERTA

Contents

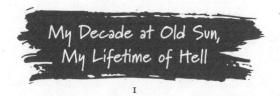

Preface

Arthur and I had our final "book" meeting on a bright sunny day in September 2012. There we sat at his kitchen table, just as we had so many times before, going over certain sections of the manuscript that seemed to me to need a little more detail. After about an hour, we looked at each other and, with big smiles, together proclaimed, "It's finished!" As I drove away from Arthur's home on the Siksika reserve, I thought about our meeting and about the power of his memory—his ability not only to recall but to relive specific moments in his life and to analyze the emotions he experienced. I felt honoured, once again, to have him as a friend.

My drive back to Calgary from Siksika seemed very short. Along the way, I reflected on my nearly three-year journey of collaboration with Arthur and contemplated my one remaining task—a task that seemed unnecessary to me but that Arthur and his wife, Marie, declared essential. They expected me to write the story of the process "from the very beginning," as they said. They wanted me to present an honest account of my collaboration with Arthur.

The process began with a phone call from my good friend Marie Bear Chief on a cold grey winter morning early in 2010. Marie was a long-time "tipi holder" at the Calgary Stampede's Indian Village where I was one of many white volunteers, and Marie and I had worked together on projects relating to cultural interpretation. That morning, however, Marie did not want to talk about the Indian Village. Instead, she turned to the topic of the Siksika Nation's residential school survivors and the abuse that Arthur had experienced as a student at the Old Sun Indian Residential School. I knew from previous conversations with Marie that Arthur had received a settlement for the abuses he had suffered at the school, but this was the first time that she spoke of sexual abuse. Yes, Arthur had been sexually abused, and he wanted to make his experience public by writing a book about his life. As Marie explained, Arthur had asked her whether she knew anybody who might be able to provide a little help, and she had picked me. She said that she trusted me and that Arthur would trust me too. Now that was quite a compliment, but I wondered whether I could truly be of assistance. Would Arthur really be able to trust a woman with such a personal story?

But, since Marie seemed convinced that he would, I tucked my concerns away and focused my thoughts on Arthur, the writer. I did not question his abilities at all. I had first heard of Arthur many years earlier from Leo

Youngman, the former chief of the Siksika Nation. In the late 1980s, Leo spearheaded the development of Blackfoot Crossing Historical Park, and, as a heritage planner for the Province of Alberta, I had the honour of working with him for many years. In 1989, with the help of funding from the province, Leo hired his son-in-law, whom he described as a man worthy only of the highest respect and an individual with considerable experience in the civil service, for a six-month term as project administrator. Leo insisted that I meet Arthur, so at the start of his term position, he and I shook hands, and, at the end, we spoke once on the phone. Arthur and I did not recognize each other when Marie introduced us at the Indian Village well over a decade later, and I said nothing to Marie about my earlier encounter with him. But at least then I knew which of Leo's daughters had married the man Leo had called "important."

Marie went on to ask whether I knew anything about how to secure a publisher in order to make Arthur's book available to the Siksika community and the general public. The only person who came to mind—someone who knew publishing and could, I felt, be trusted with Arthur's story—was Frits Pannekoek, an historian with a background in Indigenous cultural heritage. When we spoke, he volunteered to help. Suffice it to say that before noon on that gloomy winter day, I was able to call Arthur and let him know that he had both a helper and the support of someone who was enthusiastic about the book and could advise him about finding a publisher.

Arthur talked about his writing process and why he had asked for assistance: simply put, this was the first time he had attempted writing a book, and he was not sure whether what he'd written was "publisher-ready." We agreed to meet at his house, so that he, Marie, and I could discuss the project and Arthur could give me copies of what he had written. During our next phone conversation, Arthur summarized his residential school experiences, including some graphic descriptions of abuse. My worries about whether he would trust me vanished. Arthur Bear Chief is a powerful storyteller, and his words, even at this early stage, affected me deeply. The "very beginning" of the project was complete.

Shortly thereafter, I sat down with Arthur and Marie to learn more about the book and why Arthur wanted to write it. I left with copies of Arthur's writings and my promise to do a little rearranging and minor editing before sending the material to Frits. Those initial writings revealed Arthur's very compelling style of storytelling, one that evoked in me a wide range of emotional responses, as well as a genuine interest in his life's story.

At the end of April, after Frits had reviewed Arthur's first draft, the four of us gathered around the Bear Chief kitchen table to discuss the book and an outline that Frits had drawn up. Frits appreciated the author's storytelling skills and writing abilities, and he asked me to send Arthur's future writings directly to him. We met again in late August to finalize the book's structure, and Arthur agreed to fill in a few blank spaces in his story and to expand other passages by supplying some additional description.

In working with Arthur, I was constantly amazed by his memory—by all the details that came back to him.

The vivid descriptions that he provided of his horrific experiences at Old Sun Residential School became almost palatable for me because of the anecdotes he told about the occasional bright spots in his life. For example, Arthur truly loved the bowl of chocolate pudding that students were given every Sunday. When he described the delight he took in that weekly bowl of chocolate pudding, his eyes sparkled, and I caught a glimpse of the spirit of hope and resilience that allowed him to survive those years. Some four decades later, Arthur made the courageous decision to take his story of abuse into the justice system. The emotional pain he had to endure in order to win his settlement was hard for me to imagine, but I paid close attention to his every word, and I distinctly remember that, as he came to the end of the story, he said in a matter-of-fact voice, "And I had to pay GST." The way he said it made me laugh first, but when I asked, "You're kidding, right?" he replied with a simple "No." These two symbols—chocolate pudding, representing hope, and the GST, signifying injustice—will remain forever etched in both my head and my heart, and in my mind's eye, I can still see Arthur telling his story.

Arthur would call me when he had writings for Frits, and we spoke often on the telephone. Arthur has a mischievous sense of humour, and I always enjoyed the lighthearted stories he told about his past. He certainly knew how to make me laugh. Sometimes I became frustrated, though, for the simple reason that Arthur would tell me the same stories over and over and over again, from beginning to end. When he talked on the phone about new written material, the questions I had about details were set aside for with a detailed account of the meeting when I called. He said that he had enjoyed the conversation, but his voice sounded slightly subdued and perhaps a bit sad. I asked Arthur whether something was wrong. He, in turn, asked me whether I had looked at the edited draft and then said that he was not sure about it. After admitting that I hadn't even had a chance to look at it, I asked him, with some trepidation, what he meant. When he explained his uncertainty about some of the ways his original had been changed, all it took to cheer him up was, "Ah, it is revision time. I'm sure Frits will welcome changes and comments."

I arranged to meet with Arthur so that we could talk further about his doubts and work out a plan for revision. At our meeting, Arthur pointed to sections in the draft where his voice seemed to be almost lost, and he asked why some significant events were not included as he had intended. "Frits did not have the advantage of hearing you, Arthur, like I did," I replied. "I know your stories inside out because I heard them so often from you, and I know where the many parts fit within the whole." I then attempted to suggest some methods that Arthur could use to get the revision process underway. He was not receptive, but he did want to talk about the examination for discovery that he had to undergo in connection with his lawsuit. This interrogation took place on two consecutive days in October 2002, with a follow-up day in February 2003. As he spoke about the ordeal, Arthur could not hide his tears, and I sat motionless, spellbound by his words. I was beginning to understand, in my heart, the depth of his pain and how difficult it must have been for him to testify about what happened to him longer treated me as a fellow human being. Not only did he imply that I was fully responsible for what he perceived to be a lack of progress, but he also made me feel like a simple household tool that could be used if needed and otherwise ignored or simply thrown out. During this difficult time, although I never said as much, I often thought, "What a jerk!"

Even though Arthur seemed unwilling to recognize it, we actually were making progress. While I had accepted the responsibility for entering changes in the manuscript, I refused to revise anything without his full participation. But, during our meetings, he seemed to forget that we had already agreed on what each section of the book should include and that we had developed a useful system for working through the second draft. He also appeared to have forgotten the interesting and enjoyable conversations we used to have at the end of our meetings. My resentment at being perceived as nothing more than a well-worn tool even made it hard for me to take an interest in Arthur's fond memories about his time as a judo champion and trainer, first in Ontario and later in Saskatchewan. If nothing else, though, I was beginning to understand why Arthur sometimes chose to make extremely negative comments about himself in his narrative: he was just being honest.

I finally came to the end of my patience during a phone call from an angry Arthur making yet another demand on my time. I was just too busy for him that day, so I abruptly ended the conversation. "I will call you when I have time," I told him. The only reason I refrained from saying, "Go to hell!" was the fact that Marie had asked me to help. I felt obligated to her, but not to her grumpy husband.

I gave myself a few weeks to get over my angry, hurt feelings before I phoned Arthur back. To my relief, he sounded like the cheerful friend whose company I enjoyed, and we promptly set up our next work session. Arthur gave me a happy greeting when I arrived, and we immediately got back to work on our review of the draft. The method we both liked was simple: Arthur read the draft aloud to me, and I listened. If either one of us had an issue, we stopped the reading and had a discussion. Together we would make a decision on the required revision, and I would then make a note of it. I remember that, during one session, I began to feel distressed and asked Arthur if we could stop. He looked at me and agreed. Why I almost began crying is a mystery to me: we were nearing the end of the manuscript, and it had not affected me in this way before. "Arthur, this must be so hard for you," I said. He responded with, "Yes. Yes, it is." As I look back on that meeting, I think that perhaps I had finally come to understand the real Arthur and why he so badly wanted the book to be finished.

As we moved towards the final stages of the revision process, Arthur began to tell me new stories, many of them light-hearted, but he chose not to include most of these in the book. "My life is more than just Old Sun," he said. "But my writing is about the effects of residential school on my life. These stories do not fit." I understood what he meant. I sometimes felt that I had become his personal repository of memories. At one point, I told him, "Arthur, I believe I know more about your life than any other human being."

He did not disagree. While at times I found it difficult to know so much, I never doubted that it was an honour to be entrusted with these memories.

Arthur's book is worthy of a slow, thoughtful reading. My journey with him was a bumpy one, but it was well worth the trip. His courage and wisdom will always be with me, and I know he is a true friend who will always have a lesson to share if I pay attention to the stories he tells.

Judy Bedford

Acknowledgements

There are three people whom I wish to acknowledge who helped make my dream a reality. Judy Bedford, who worked diligently alongside me in putting my stories in the proper order and in editing the countless drafts of my manuscript. Frits Pannekoek, for his expertise, his research, his afterword, and his knowledge of the book business. My wife, Marie, who said to me, "Get your butt moving and quit procrastinating" and whose strong belief in me pushed me to write this book. I am forever indebted to these people.

My Decade at Old Sun,
My Lifetime of Hell

I am sitting here tonight—three days before Christmas in 2010—alone in my basement. Nobody wants to have anything to do with me because I have been drinking. Before my wife left the house, she told me, "I don't want to take you. All you're going to do is drink." So, once again, I am left by myself because I am not wanted. I have messed up so badly in my life that I cannot even be a father or a husband to anyone.

I screwed up so bad with life. Why am I still here? I can't do anything right. I wish someone would just kill me, like they do with wounded animals. It would put me out of the misery I have lived with for so long. I just wanted to be part of everything. I cannot be perfect in everything I do, but I try to do my best.

I am crying, but I do not wish to take my own life for it is wrong to take life when it is such a great gift from God. I have been hurt so much so much in life. I feel so inadequate about myself. Why can't someone come forward to give me a hug just the way Mother used to hug me? Simply that would make me feel wanted and loved. I did not ask to be this way. I just wanted to be normal like everybody else, and for that I get punished for life for what I went through. Nobody should have to go through what I went through.

The suicidal thoughts of that Christmas-time evening don't happen all the time now, but that night was similar to many others when I've been home alone. I have real good conversations with my best buddy, Coors Light, who never condemns me or is critical of my actions. Coors Light just listens to me with no back talk. He is the only one who seems to understand how I feel, and when the scenes from residential school start going like a TV screen, he doesn't mind that I cry like a baby. He doesn't say a word. He lets me wonder why no one is around to hug me and kiss me on the forehead and say, "There, there, Art, everything is going to be all right. Mommy is here to protect you from harm and danger."

But the harm and danger have already taken a toll, both physically and emotionally, and the tears keep coming like a waterfall. They seem endless, but then, like a bolt of lightning, I come back to reality, and I say to myself, "What the hell are you crying about you fucking big baby? Nobody is going to help you. Grow up and take it like a man, just like you have always done before! You are alone in this fight, so get used to it. No one is going to give you any tender loving care. Mommy is gone, so be brave and fight on for yourself." When I am through scolding myself, I take a deep breath and have another beer to soothe the pain I have inside of me.

As I look back on my life, I find myself laughing at it, swearing at it, and feeling some fondness for some aspects of it. My life is like a cocoon that never really hatched. I was prevented from becoming a full-fledged butterfly with all its natural beauty. I remember the happiness and the joy of being young and surrounded by adults who cared for and loved me. And then I was forced to enter residential school, and I get angry and bitter about what I lost, and I feel a lot of pain. I drink to forget this pain, but with each sip, the pain seems to grow bigger inside of me. It's almost like some kind of disease eating away at my innards, but I carry on battling my demons and recognize that I am lucky to have the family I have now and that I carry with me the spirit of my culture and traditions.

I, Arthur Bear Chief, owe my resilience to our ancestors and elders for instilling in me a spirit strong enough to survive what I went through in residential school. We survivors left the residential schools with so many scars that we would carry for the rest of our lives. Eventually these scars would lead many of us to an early death. A few of us managed to prosper in careers, to live a comfortable life and raise a family, but this wasn't because of anything we were taught in residential school. It was a testament to our Indian spirit and our determination to overcome obstacles even in the most difficult situations. I praise my ancestors and grandparents for giving me both. The schools may have beaten us physically and emotionally, but we came out with the same spirit that our ancestors instilled in us so many years past. I once heard an old saying, which is still true: "You may beat us, break our bones. Then you can have my dead body, but not my obedience."

When I look back to my first year at Old Sun Indian Residential School, I remember standing outside the washroom located in our playroom. Reverend Cole, along with the farm boss, Mr. Fraser, with the strap in his hand, waited for the big boys to come out of the washroom. Fraser would lay at least four or five straps on each boy's hand, but they showed no pain on their faces. They simply walked away with a smirk, as if this was an everyday thing they had endured in the past. Looking back now, I can almost see the spirit of our ancestors sparkling in their eyes. Today, their reaction makes me proud of my Indian heritage and the resilience that comes with it. These older boys taught me something early on in residential school, and that is to hang onto my courage and spirit no matter what obstacles are put in front of me.

I almost lost the Indian spirit in me when I left the reserve in the sixties. I thank my ancestors for not turning their backs on me. I can almost see it like it was yesterday at a powwow, when an elder stands up with a blanket wrapped around his waist, dances in one spot, raises an eagle feather in one hand and hoots. What a powerful spirit!

Sometimes I wonder if my child's spirit is still waiting for me to take it back home to settle into the life that was so comfortable and good before we were taken away from home so long ago. I still cry in silence when I think of all those years in that place, so alone and scared, wondering what's going to happen next—yearning for my mother's touch and hug like it used to be. That will only ever come back in my dreams. How sad for me to be denied the right to have a normal childhood upbringing.

I am writing this book in hopes that it will help me in my journey of healing and recovery from my abuse at Old Sun Residential School. Everything else I have attempted eventually led me back to myself without any resolution to rid me of my demons. My emotions still overtake me at times, and I sit and cry for myself and many others who are not here—gone, but not forgotten by me. May your spirits guide me in the writing of my book. If your spirit is restless, I hope this book will give you some sense of peace. If that is the case, I too will be at peace with you.

When I go back to the days before residential school, I think very fondly of the memories of my mother. She used to touch my face and give me a little hug, just a little reassurance of her love. This may seem inconsequential to many, but it meant a lot to me at that time. To be denied this is what was so fundamentally wrong with the residential schools. Chief Dan George said in *My Heart Soars*, "There have been times when we all wanted so desperately to feel a reassuring hand upon us . . . there have been lonely times when we so wanted a strong arm around us." This is so true. In my first years at the Old Sun school, I would run out to the prairie to cry because I felt so lonely. I can still feel the pain when I talk about it. My tears come with no encouragement. They just naturally flow. How I wish so many times that I could go back to my childhood just to feel the loving touch of my mother's hands. It was so unfair.

Dan George says, "We all must have love to live. It nurtures us and gives us the feeling of being wanted and cared for. Love is something you and I must have. We must have it because our spirit feeds upon it. We must have it because without it we become weak and faint. Without love our self-esteem weakens. Without it our courage fails. Without love we can no longer look out confidently at the world. Instead we turn inwardly and begin to feed upon our own personalities and little by little we destroy ourselves." The lack of love I got at Old Sun Indian Residential School turned me out into the world as an uncaring, unloving, cold, emotionless individual with no understanding of what love meant. My alcoholism and the demons inside of me have been destroying me little by little. In the end, this may well be my demise. This is a true testimony of what the residential schools did to me personally. How can I honestly say that I forgive you for what you did to me? I am so bitter and angry at many things. It is hard for me to move on because I can't. The past has yet to be cleansed from my memory.

I was born on the Blackfoot Indian Reserve #146 on June 25, 1942, at the old Blackfoot hospital. My parents, Walker and Martha Bear Chief, were married on November 26, 1933. They had a total of twelve children, and I was number five:

Wallace	1934		Old Sun
Francis	1935–2007	Pale Coloured Rider	Old Sun
Clement	1938	One Who Shines in the Dark	Old Sun (high school in Cluny and Cardston)
Donna	1940	Holy Crow Woman	Old Sun (high school in Edmonton)
Arthur	1942	Big Wolf	Old Sun
Joan	1944	Good Shining Woman	Old Sun (high school in Cluny and Carseland)
Melvin	1946	First Among Riders	Old Sun (high school in Drumheller)
Roy	1948	Many Wives	Old Sun (high school in Cluny)
Alvina	1950	Underground Woman	Old Sun (high school in Carseland)
Celeste	1952		Gleichen Public School
Robert	1954	Nicknamed "Mohawk"	Gleichen Public School
Patsy	1956		Gleichen Public School

My parents had also attended residential school on the reserve, my father going to Old Sun and my mother to the Crowfoot Indian Residential School. They did not participate much in our traditional culture. But they did have my oldest brother raised by his grandparents when he was a youngster, and I remember them singing some of our traditional songs. I also know that my father eventually sold off his parents' Indian artifacts.

My mother stayed at home with the young kids, while my father went off to work. First, he worked as a farm hand, but by the time I was born, he was employed by the Imperial Oil Company in Calgary. Then he worked for the Gleichen flour mill, and in 1949 he began working as an interpreter for the Department of Indian Affairs at the Blackfoot Indian Agency. He moved up in the hierarchy of the department and stayed there until he retired.

My paternal grandparents were William and Minnie Bear Chief. Their Blackfoot names were Gull Chief and Man Killer. The story I heard about my grandfather is that he was found by a member of the North-West Mounted Police out on the prairies during a snow storm. The officer, James Stanford, took him to Montana when he left the force, and my grandfather was raised by James's mother until he turned eighteen. Then he got on a stage to come back to Alberta to visit his own mother. But instead of returning to Montana, he stayed at Siksika and married Minnie Dog Child, who was from the Blood tribe. He joined the NWMP and stayed with the force for ten years. After he left the force in 1915, he raised cattle and took up farming. Grandfather Bear Chief died in

1943 at the age of eighty-one. I was still a baby when he passed away, so I never knew him. But Grandmother Bear Chief, who later took up with Peter Little Light, I knew very well. She lived to the age of eighty-nine, passing away in 1960.

My maternal grandparents were Black Kettle and Mary Black Kettle. I know nothing about my grandfather; he died long before I was born. Grandmother Mary was born at North Battleford, Saskatchewan. Her Blackfoot name was One Night Alone, and her father was a white man. I know that she had one sister, Mrs. Ida Inkster, who homesteaded in the North Battleford region. When she was still a baby, Mary returned to Siksika with her mother. With Black Kettle, Grandmother Mary had three children, Francis, Nicholas, and Martha, my mother. After the death of Black Kettle, she married Heavy Shield, who I spent much time with when I was a young boy.

Prior to entering Old Sun Indian Residential School on September 1, 1949, I was perhaps like any normal Indian child, nurtured and loved by my parents, grandparents, and aunts and uncles. We all spoke Blackfoot, and I remember being happy. Severe punishment was unheard of, but reprimands for bad behaviour were stern. We did not have many material things, but our family was caring and complete in every sense.

We were not rich, but we always had food to eat. Mind you, it was not steak every night, but a lot of fried bread and fried potatoes, and of course, Indian steak—baloney. I also liked peanut butter and jam, especially when I got a sandwich from my aunt, Mabel Bear Chief, who had three girls, Maggie, Peggy, and Amy, who were all raised by William and Minnie Bear Chief. Auntie Mabel used to stay with Old Man Paul Fox, who lived over at the Old Crowfoot Dance Hall. I used to sneak over to their place from my house at the "Four Houses." I would knock on the door, and my auntie would answer. I can still hear Old Man Fox asking, "Who is that?" My auntie would say my Indian name, and he would give a little laugh and say, "Come for his snack." Auntie Mabel would fix me a peanut butter and jam sandwich and pour me a cold glass of milk. When I finished, I returned the glass, and my Auntie Mabel and Paul would walk me out and watch me as I got to the other road. I would look back and wave to both of them. They would wave back and then go inside. I would start to run to head for home.

Of course, my mother always scolded me for going away without telling her, and she would also often throw in the words "begging again." Mother used to tell Mabel, "I keep telling him not to go to your place. He always goes there to beg!" My auntie, in such a loving voice, would say, "Never mind. He comes to visit us, and I give him a treat. We enjoy him."

I never worried too much about the scolding because Mother was always there to give me her affection. I remember times when I was playing by myself and suddenly felt I needed a little tender loving touch. I would run to my mother, grab her around her legs, and wait for her to gently touch my face and say to me, "Mother loves you." Then I would run away to play again. Those gentle moments with my mother gave me the feeling of having a strong bond between us that I never thought would be broken.

I remember we used to have my cousins Mabel and Noella Black Kettle stay with us at the Four Houses during clean-up time. The floors were scrubbed and waxed. When the wax was dry, my cousins would be given a gunny sack to polish the floor. They would sit me on the sack and slide me all over the floor. Boy, was that ever fun for me! And the floor was very shiny.

I remember a story my late brother Francis told me. I apparently had a bad habit of going to bed with some bannock. I used to put it into my mouth and suck it like a baby and fall asleep, eventually spitting it out. Well, one night I guess I was doing my normal routine when my brother Francis was lying beside me. All of a sudden I spit the well-used bannock into the air, and it came down directly on my brother's face. He was so disgusted that he took the bannock and smacked it right back on my face. Of course, I was oblivious to all that because I was fast asleep. From what I was told, it got so bad that nobody wanted to sleep with me.

When my father worked at the flour mill in Gleichen, we moved to Old Man Low Horn's place during the spring and summer. We pitched a tent and stayed there so my father would have only a short distance to walk to his job. I remember being with Low Horn and his grandchildren. The old man would sit all of us in front of him and tell us old-time stories. Low Horn was so gentle and loving that I never saw him get mad at us for any reason, and I remember he used to tell the adults, "Children are our pride and future. Treat them with gentleness and patience, and don't ever punish them physically, but set them straight." Yes, my family life was filled with love and positive interaction with adults.

I was very fortunate to have been able to spend considerable time with both sets of grandparents. I spent days and sometimes weeks with them, and they taught me the beginnings of my true culture, although as a young boy, I always thought it was cutting into my playtime. Little did I know that this was supposed to be a very important part of learning our customs and culture.

The times I spent with my grandparents gave me many memories. I remember one summer when my sister Donna and I were staying with Grandmother Mary and Heavy Shield. The Old Man, who was a bundle holder and a member of the Horn Society, had a lot of interesting items that he would take to the Calgary Stampede. I remember his old flintlock gun and a tomahawk with a big oval rock tied with leather to a wooden handle. It was heavy, and it was a definite challenge for me to try and lift it. Much to my frustration, I could never do it. Old Man Heavy Shield used to sit on his bed and watch with great amusement at my struggles with that tomahawk.

After supper, before I went to bed, Heavy Shield would get out his drum and start to sing. He would invite me to join him, and he encouraged me to dance. Of course, I much enjoyed doing my best imitation of a World Chicken Dance champion. Heavy Shield would tell my Grandma Mary, "Look at our boy. He is going to be a great dancer." Grandma Mary would say, "I am going to help my son." She would put a blanket around her waist, dance in one spot, and raise her hand and wave it around. What a wonderful memory!

I remember one summer before my sister Donna entered residential school. We were staying with Grandma Mary and Heavy Shield, and we had to go out and gather roots and other plants. Only my Grandma knew where to look and dig. Being young, Donna and I were not interested in those types of exploration. When Grandma finished her work, we would return to the house. I asked her what the roots were for. She said, "It's for my medicine." I didn't think too much about it until one time when I had a terrible eye infection. Heavy Shield said to my Grandma, "I think it's time you doctor our boy. His eye looks real bad." My Grandma told me to lie on her bed, and she got out her bag and took something from it. She chewed it, and with all the juice from the root, she spit it into my eye. Boy did that sting! She covered my eye, and when she removed the patch that evening, my eye was cured. It was perfect with no redness in the eyeball.

Another time when we were seeking roots and picking berries, Donna and I started throwing sticks at a bee hive. Just as our grandmother came walking by, a bee came out of the hive and stung her on the side of her head, on the cheek bone, which resulted in a large swelling. We were killing ourselves laughing at her. She never said anything or scolded us. As we headed back to the car, she looked at us and burst out laughing at herself.

One time Old Man Heavy Shield parked his car on the side of a small hill but forgot to put on the handbrake. We didn't notice that the car had started to roll down the hill. My grandmother Mary ran after it, holding the car on driver's side and hollering, "Whoa! Whoa!" Grandfather Heavy Shield was killing himself laughing, saying to her, "The car cannot hear you." Of course, the car did not stop until it reached the bottom. No damage or harm was done, except to my grandmother's pride. I think she felt stupid.

One other time, Donna and I were sitting in the back of Heavy Shield's car, heading towards Gleichen, a treat for us. It was quite windy and hot, so naturally all the car windows were open. My Grandma was clearing her chest of mucus, and she spit out a great big glob. The wind caught it, and it came back in through the rear window and landed on my sister's face. She was sitting there crying "Grandma!" and, of course, Grandma turned around in her seat and tried to clean my sister's face. The Old Man and I were busting our guts laughing. He had to stop the car for everyone to collect themselves before we could continue on our journey.

Sometimes Donna and I stayed with Grandma Bear Chief. When we were ready for bed, Grandma Bear Chief would sit beside us on the makeshift bed on the floor.

Donna would say, "Tell us a story." She would begin by singing a song for us and then tell the story. Eventually I guess we fell to sleep. To this day, I still miss my grandma's gentleness and her gentle rocking when she held me. What love!

I remember one time when our step-grandfather, Little Light, was going to open his medicine bundle, which he kept in the bedroom of their two-room house. Other elders were invited to witness the ceremony. I was instructed by Grandma Bear Chief to sit on the outside of the circle and look and listen. I was not very appreciative of this because I was missing out on my playing time. I did not realize that this was the start of my training in our culture.

Grandma Bear Chief once took me to a Tobacco Dance. I hardly remember anything about this ceremony, but one story stayed with me. When we broke camp to head home, I was instructed to not look back towards the camp. I did not know why, but the story I heard about this taboo was that sticks shaped like humans were put into the ground. Why I don't really know, but the story goes on to say that one individual did look back and saw those sticks come to life and dance.

I was also privileged to have been at a Ghost Dance with Grandma Bear Chief at Old Man Jack Kip's residence at North Camp. During one of the dances, Grandma placed my head under a blanket and instructed me not to look up. However, when you are young, you want to see what's going on, so I took a peek, and what I saw I really don't understand. I saw figures covered completely by something dancing to the rhythm of the drumming. I quickly covered my head again, and I never asked my Grandma for an explanation about what I saw.

One summer, Grandma Bear Chief and Little Light went by wagon to the Blood reserve for their annual Sun Dance. They took along another old lady, Mrs. Gunny Crow. While in transit, I must have been sleeping with one foot dangling over the side of the wagon. My shoe fell off and was lost, but Old Lady Gunny Crow made moccasins for me to wear during the remainder of the trip. At the end of the Sun Dance, I had my face painted by the sun woman, and that night when I was playing with another boy, we got into a fight. He scratched up my face pretty good, and of course I went crying to my grandma. While she was cleaning my face, Old Lady Gunny Crow gave me the name Crazy Youngman. This was my second Indian name.

I want to share one other story that I remember about my brother Francis before I entered residential school. My brother Melvin and my sister Joan and I were sitting in the front room when Francis came running into the house, jumped up to the attic opening, and crawled inside the attic. Not long after that, three white men and an RCMP officer came running in. They dragged my brother down as he was screaming and kicking. They dragged him out, and my parents could not do anything. That was a preview of what was in store for me.

Little did I know that a very dark and sinister cloud was fast approaching to whisk me away to a place I knew nothing about, and that it would scar me for the rest of my life. Yes, I was about to get a rude awakening. My mother told me that somebody came at the end of June 1949, when I turned seven, to pick me up and take me to Old Sun Indian Residential School. But since it was the end of the school year, I was only there for two days. It was in September that residential school took over my childhood.

Those of us who attended residential school, particularly those of us who went in September and did not see or have contact with our parents until the school year ended in June of the following year, are the survivors who suffered the deepest feelings of rejection, anger, and low self-esteem. Many of us lost our childhoods, those precious years when we should have been bonding with and nurtured by our parents. Instead we were sent to residential school and subjected to very harsh and cruel treatment and living conditions. We grew up fast and hard, deprived of the pleasures of normal loving parents, grandparents, and extended families. We were forced to become adults very quickly. I get angry knowing that this fundamental right for all families in Canada was denied to us as First Nations people simply because of government policies.

It was not fair or humane to us survivors who lost our childhood during our most formative years when you are supposed to become self-assured and proud of who you are instead of hanging your head about yourself. I do not have childhood memories of school that are fond and loving.

Instead, I remember the beatings and punishments and the fear inside of me, making me wish I was not there. I often wish it was all just a bad dream rather than the nightmares that stayed with me for many years.

As a child growing up in residential school when I should have been enjoying my childhood playing with siblings and friends, I was left alone to fend for myself. Many times I was alone out in the field crying for some tender loving touch, just for someone to hug me because I was lonely and scared. But no one ever came to comfort me. I never had the opportunity to run to my mother when I got hurt while playing so I could be comforted and hugged and reassured that everything was going to be all right because mother was there to protect me from harm. No, I did not know such tenderness while growing up in residential school. I grew from a child into a teenager without ever fully knowing how to be a child. Instead, I became a man in a child's body, with so many dysfunctions that my future was bleak and uncertain. I was not adequately nurtured to go into the real world because the only life I really knew was residential school.

I would give anything to take this life back and to be able to enjoy it and feel what it's really like to be a child. It was so unfair on the government's part because of their policies regarding Indians living on reserves. I lost so much as a child. How can anyone put a price to it and simply say, "Sorry, we were wrong. It should not have happened"? I sometimes wonder whether the government learned anything from this dark era. I do not think so. So my lost childhood is simply part of a chapter on how government policies failed. What about me and so many others who were cheated out of our childhoods? I guess we're just supposed to suck it up and move on.

I was seven years old when I entered Old Sun in September of 1949. I did not speak English, nor did I understand it. I was scared out of my wits. That first night, when we were marched upstairs to our dorm, I simply followed the rest of the boys and did what they did, like taking your clothes off, folding them and placing them at the foot of your bed, and, after that, putting on your pajamas and then kneeling down on the floor and praying. When we completed that, we crawled into bed. Once the lights were out, I got scared, and I started to cry for my mother. The supervisor, Miss Twigg, came and started yelling at me, which I did not understand. When I didn't stop crying, she went back to her room and came back with something and said something to me. When my crying did not stop, she started hitting me with something. She kept on hitting me, not stopping. I finally curled up into a fetal position, grabbed the pillow, and bit into it to muffle my crying. Only then did she stop hitting me.

The next morning, I was told by the older boys never to cry for my mother or I would get the same punishment. From that point on, I realized that crying would mean getting a beating. My early years in Old Sun Indian Residential School generally consisted of half a day of school and half a day of work. When this stopped, I can't remember.

I remember the male supervisor who used to make the boys form a human ring. I was forced to fight. They wrapped my hands in towels, and the other boy's too, and then we would have to slug it out. We would both be crying, but he would not stop the fight until one of us had a bleeding nose or a cut. Who was the savage here?

The female supervisor we had, Miss Twigg, was mean and did things I did not understand, like we had to massage her with our hands, and she just lay on the bed moaning. The other thing is, after we showered, she lined us up. We would have to lift our pajamas and expose our penises. Then, one by one, she pulled back the foreskins and looked at them. When she completed that, we would be allowed to get into bed after our prayers.

I only remember one night when that massaging ritual did not occur. A crew from Crawley Films came to Old Sun during my first year to film the daily activities of our lives. Everything was staged, including our bedtime preparations. That night the junior boys were given cookies to eat and a glass of milk as we sat on our beds. I really enjoyed the bedtime snack, and I did not miss at all the act of massaging Miss Twigg!

Punishments varied. I had to stand for over an hour at attention, not moving or it would be longer. By the time the hour was up, we would almost be peeing in our pants and would all make a mad dash to the bathroom. Every evening, we all would go to church, and if for some reason the minister did not like the way we came up the stairs, we would have to march from the playroom to the church and back down again. This could last for over an hour. As a very young boy, this was physically excruciatingly painful for me. By the time it ended, we, the junior boys, were ready to go to bed. We would barely make it up the stairs and go through the ritual of massaging our supervisor, and then we'd hit the hay and be out like a light.

There were times when I would go out to the field by myself and sit there calling for my mother. There, all by myself with no one to hold me or cuddle me, I sat and cried until all my tears dried up. Only then would I return to the play area. We were shown no love or affection by anyone, period. Never a touch to indicate that everything was going to be all right. The ultimate betrayal was that we could not turn to our parents. This is what hurts the most. Every one of us had parents, but they were denied their right to be our parents.

Sometimes when I was upstairs in our dorm, I'd look out the windows towards my home at the Four Houses, where I could see my mother out in the yard. I secretly cried and wished she could be beside me to stroke me on the head and face and tell me, "Mother loves you." Why was this denied to me? I did not understand why I was deprived of family, home, and all the love I knew before. As far as I can remember, we never celebrated Thanksgiving, Halloween, and Christmas or Easter, and birthdays were unheard of. Consequently, they were not very important to me later on in my years.

Church was very important, though, so every Sunday parents came to our services. They had to sit in the back, and we were not allowed to turn and look at them. We just had to sit straight and look forward. If you did look, you would be punished severely for that. When the service finished, the parents would file out, and we would have to sit until they were all out of the building. Only then would we be allowed to leave the chapel, return to our dorms, and change clothes. They were so close, but so far away.

In my first full year of school, I was told by the boys that my brother Francis wanted to talk to me. He was locked in a broom closet just outside the laundry room. I went there, and he told me he was hungry and to steal bread for him. Without fear, I went to the school bakery and stole a loaf of bread, then ran back to him, and ripped it apart to shove through the tiny openings. He told me to run before anyone came. I ran outside to the field and sat down to cry for my brother; I did not understand why he was being locked in the broom closet without food. I sat there wondering why there was no help for us, and I cried out for my mother to help Francis and me. But my cries were never heard. Many times, alone, out somewhere where no one would see me, I cried, longing for my mother's touch and tender pat on the head. I would go to bed aching for a tender loving touch that never came. How cruel and unfair!

I remember playing in our playroom once. I saw Miss Twigg standing there. I was so starved for love that I ran to her and grabbed her legs like I used to do with my mother, who would pat my head and face and say, "I love you." Then I would run away to play. Well, that did not happen. Instead I got a good beating from her in front of everyone. Nobody would or could help me. So instead of crying, I held everything in. I ran outside to the field where I cried. I could not understand the treatment. I was scared constantly, not knowing when I would get another beating.

When I came home that first summer, in 1950, I was playing in the front room of our house. I can still remember my mother and Mrs. Crane Bear talking. Mrs. Not Useful and Mrs. Yellow Horse and some other elderly ladies were also present. They were talking in hushed tones when, in a very loud voice, my mother said, "Same with me. My son (she called me by my Indian name) has changed so much. What did they do to him? They must have really mistreated him." In her heart, she knew I had changed and was not the same person who was sent away to school. My mother's comments that day have stayed with me all my life.

When I first entered residential school, we had vegetable and potato gardens that had to be harvested in the fall every year. So, in my first full year, I had to work in the potato field. It was backbreaking work; to be precise, it was child slave labour. It had to be done from sun-up to almost sun-down, and then it was back to school for supper and evening prayers, and to bed to start over the next day until it was all done. I had never known such hard labour in my short life. But I had to grin and bear it.

I was about eleven or twelve years old when I had to milk cows. I'd get up at about 4:00 in the morning and head over to the barn to prepare the cows for milking. When that was done, we had to return the full jerry cans to the creamery, ready for separation. After breakfast, if you can call it that, we went back to clean the stalls of shit and straw, wash them out, and cart out all the shit to the manure pile. What a shitty job, but you had to do it.

Meals left a lot to be desired. We never had much, but, every Sunday, we used to get chocolate pudding. Oh boy, we used to look forward to that! I and others, I am sure, so looked forward to tasting our one and only luxury. I used to prolong finishing it so I could enjoy tasting every bit of it. I would have licked the bowl, but doing that would have risked a beating. That was not an option.

Sometimes, when we got up in the morning, we could smell burnt porridge in our dorm. When we went down to breakfast, some of us could not eat it. The supervisor came around with an oil can with a spout to squirt cod liver oil in your mouth. If you gagged on it, he would squirt it into your porridge, and you would be forced to eat it at lunchtime.

I witnessed a lot of punishments at Old Sun. Reverend Cole, the administrator, was a very mean individual who enjoyed hurting us. He came from England, where he had played a lot of soccer. He could kick a soccer ball like a gun releases a bullet. There were times when we were playing in the playroom, and he would come in with a soccer ball and kick it right at us. We had to run from side to side to avoid getting hit, but some of us were not so lucky. He would do this until he got tired and left. Once I got hit on the head and was knocked out cold.

I recall that when I first entered Old Sun, all the students were in the dining room, eating. Reverend Cole came in and called a girl to come forward. He immediately grabbed her and pulled her dress up and pulled her panties down and began strapping her. How can a man of the cloth do that with absolutely no regard for her dignity? But then there was no dignity on their part.

Once, my friend, my cousin, and I were playing in one of the two bathtubs in our washroom beside the playroom. One of the boy's rubber boots was muddy, so he was running the water and pretending he was skiing. Reverend Cole came in out of nowhere and slapped him so hard that he knocked him out of the bathtub. His scream scared me so much that I ran out to hide. When I finally went to find him, his eyeball was red. He couldn't stop crying, so I stayed with him until his crying stopped.

Another time we were all in the playroom and had been told not to go outside. But my cousin wanted to sneak outside, so I agreed to go with him. As we were going back in, Mr. Cole came out with his flashlight. I managed to run and hide, and all I heard was a loud slap. My cousin let out a scream. Mr. Cole did not see me. I waited for a while and then went back inside, where I found my cousin crying with one eyeball completely red. Injuries like that were never taken care of. You just went on.

Bill Starr, our supervisor, used to bring a boy who used to wet his bed down to the playroom along with his wet sheets and make him wash them. Other times he would force him to drink a cup of cocoa with something in it that he claimed was a dead mouse. When he refused, Mr. Starr would literally force it down the boy's throat. He would kick and scream and cry. We all stood there watching during this cruel treatment, but none of us could do anything about it. I could not even cry for him because I knew it was not going to help.

I remember one time Bill Starr punished me and others for something I cannot now remember. We were forced to scrub the playroom floor with only a bowl, a chunk of soap, a small rectangular cloth, about three inches square, and a tooth brush. We scrubbed until about three o'clock in the morning to get about halfway finished. That was when he allowed us to go upstairs to sleep. It was excruciatingly painful. None of us could stand straight; our backs were killing us. But it didn't matter to him. He made his point, and I got it for sure.

He was a sadist who used to fashion all kinds of different straps, big and small, which he used on us for speaking Blackfoot. I am proud that I can still speak my language, even though Mr. Starr tried hard to beat it out of us. Let me give you an example. As a supervisor, he had a black book with all our names in it. In fact, each staff member carried one and a coloured marker. If they caught you speaking Blackfoot, they would put a mark beside your name. We used to call Sundays "payday." Mr. Starr would strip us naked, line us up, and call out our names to say how many times we had been caught. A table with all kinds of straps represented the different colours. Depending on how many times you were caught, you would get strapped anywhere from the neck down to your bare bottom. He used these straps on us once a week, on "payday Sunday." This Sunday occurrence also showed his dark and more sinister side, and it reminds me of the old whorehouses. We were lined up naked so that he could pick his victim for that night.

I remember an incident when one of the students was punished by our teacher. I think his name was Tremane— Captain Tremane. I can't remember what the student did, but Tremane made him stand in the corner. When the student told him that he was going to tell his father about the punishment, Tremane grabbed him by the back of his hair and started to smash his face into the wall. He did not stop until the student was bloodied and crying.

Captain Tremane used to come to class in the morning, and we had to stand at attention to sing "O Canada" and salute. If we misbehaved during this morning ritual, he would tell us he was going to bring his Bren gun and kill us all. Whether the intent was real or not isn't the point; the fact is that he threatened us. As young children, we didn't understand his comments, but he scared us. He used to have a table at the back of the classroom where two older students sat because of their learning disabilities. When one of them was misbehaving or acting up, Captain Tremane would walk up to him from behind and hit him over the head with a very large book. He basically knocked him out, but the funny thing is that he didn't fall off his chair. He kept sitting there, staring ahead. Tremane shook him, and it was like he came out of a trance. Then he cried.

At one time, we had a supervisor named Robert Jones. He had a big black dog and a handgun. He didn't like anything that he took to be a challenge to his authority. When that happened, he would line us up in the playroom, stand at the door with his dog and his gun in hand, and challenge anyone who was stupid enough to try and get past him. I believe such intimidation is an offence under the criminal code, but these people got away with it because we had no way out and no one to ask for help.

An incident that occurred in the fall of 1955 finally sent Bill Starr and Reverend Cole packing. Robert Jones took us to the gym, lined us up, and called Ralph Stimson, an older student, out. I do not know what Ralph had done, nor was it explained to us. Bill Starr tried to pull his pants down so he could strap him. Ralph resisted and fought. While this was going on, Robert Jones stood there with his gun and dog and said, "Nobody make a move." Ralph put up a good fight, but eventually succumbed and got a beating that went way beyond corporal punishment. This was an assault, but no one was ever charged for it. Instead, the Indian Agent came and told all the boys that we had to vote for Bill Starr either to stay or leave. Thank God for the "yes" votes: he was gone, and, shortly after that, so was Reverend Cole.

As I said, Reverend Cole was a very mean individual. I joined the Cubs, and during one of our sessions, our leader asked us what we would like to do after Cubs. When it came to me, I told her that I wanted to quit the Cubs and join the Army Cadets, a very innocent response. But Reverend Cole had snuck into our room and heard me, and he hit me so hard on the side of the head from behind that I was knocked out cold. What reason did he have for such a brutal act? Just because I answered the question? But that does not fit into any "good reason" category.

My sexual abuse came at the hands of our supervisor, Bill Starr. It started when Nelson Wolf Leg and I had to masturbate him. He made us sit on his stomach and put his penis between our legs and pump up and down until he reached his orgasm. Then we had to spread his sperm on his chest and all over his body.

I really don't know how many boys he sexually abused when he was our supervisor since most of us would be asleep when he came in to pick his victim. I guess that was the reason he demanded that all lights be turned off so our second-storey dorm would be completely dark. Some of us were unlucky enough to be awake. We'd lay in our beds watching for him to come into our dorm. I would pull my blanket up to my chin. Then, like a ghost out of the darkness, he quietly slipped in and pulled his victim out of his bed and took him to his room. I would exhale a sigh of relief and think, "This is my lucky night," knowing full well my time would come.

I would try to figure out who the individual was. I would lay there not making a noise, and then the crying would begin from Starr's room. I tried to block it out, but it never worked. I would cover my head with the sheets and eventually fall asleep. I would wake up the next morning to go about my routine and then find someone sitting there in the playroom with some candy. I wondered to myself if that was the victim. There were a lot of these incidents, but they were never talked about. Nothing was ever said. I have blocked out so many. You forget them, but they do return at times, like a dream, and you wonder whether it was real or not.

Darkness to me represented something evil and sinister because of my abuse. I was terrified of the dark for so many years, and I don't really remember when I outgrew that fear. I had so many fears resulting from my abuse. My nightmares continued until I started counselling, and only then did they begin to fade.

I often wondered what kind of an inhumane being Bill Starr was. I know now that he would be classified as a pedophile, a sick individual who lusted after young boys, who could not defend themselves against a much stronger adult. He destroyed many lives. Many of those boys are no longer alive. I am just one who is willing to write about it so that people will know what really happened.

I guess I speak for those who are gone, who never had a chance at a life. They left this world far too young and, like me, suffered so much in silence. Many succumbed to their demons. What a shame! I always like to refer to Old Sun as a personal "hell hole." For so many of us who were unfortunate to have run across Bill Starr, it was exactly that. If all the individuals he abused came to lay criminal complaints against him, what kind of jail time would he be looking at? Would this instantly rid me of the demons that are inside of me? Would he get twenty years or only one because we are just Indians? I do know that he served time in the penitentiary at Prince Albert, Saskatchewan.

Do I seek revenge against an old man who is probably in his eighties or dead by now? In the Bible, God said, "Vengeance is mine." I feel the anger inside of me when I remember my abuse, and I wonder how many more suffered this pain and humiliation and have not spoken about it, preferring to suffer in silence. But then I say to myself, "Maybe they are dead—that's why." I do know of one individual who came out to say he was abused by Bill Starr. I cannot mention his name. It is for him to speak about his own experiences; however, he did say he forgave him. There are others I know of, but, out of respect for their families, I choose not to mention their names.

My sexual abuse went to the next level when, one night, Bill Starr came into our dorm as usual. Nelson and I were sleeping together. He pulled me from the bed. I started to cry, "Nelson, try to hold onto me!" He got a slap across the head. When Starr got me into his room, what he did to me was horrible.

I cannot remember too much. My therapist told me I have blocked out the memories. What I remember is that he tried to enter me from the rear. The pain was so great that I started to cry for him to stop. Instead he put his penis between my legs and started pumping. When he finished, he held me and whispered in my ear that he would try later. When he fell asleep, I snuck out of his room back to my bed. Nelson grabbed me, and we held onto each other, both crying. He said to me, "I will protect you." But how could he? We were not even teenagers yet, and he was probably only two years older than me.

As young boys, we didn't understand why these sexual assaults happened. What kind of a man would do such degrading things to us? Will he ever serve his full punishment? Personally, I would rather have him strapped to a wooden table in the penitentiary where I could hit him on his backside with a wooden strap. All the energy inside of me would go into every swing. When I was done, then perhaps the demons would leave my body. That would be my personal payback.

It's funny how he could be so vile but still do some good. In his last few years at Old Sun, he started a gymnastic club for senior and intermediate boys. I was one of the smaller boys. He trained us pretty good. Once we travelled to the Banff winter carnival to perform and then on to Canmore, where we performed at the local community center. There was a play we had to do. We became statues by being painted with silver paint, and we did a series of poses. When we finished, we had no shower facilities, and they had to drive us to the local mine to use its shower facilities. We felt safe because we were many, a large group.

Our last performance was at St. Paul's Indian Residential School on the Blood reserve, where we performed for the students and the public. We were actually pretty good. There was talk that we might be invited to the Calgary Stampede, but Starr was booted out before this, and it did not happen.

In the fall of 1955, after Cole and Starr left, Cannon Cook came until a new principal was found. Life in the system was actually getting better, and we were beginning to enjoy ourselves. The brutality was no longer there.

In 1956, Reverend Crocker came. He was mean, like Cole, but not to the same extreme. One of the incidents I remember was after church one Sunday. After all the parents had left the building, he called out Clifford Healy and Robert Wolf Child to come to the altar individually.

He just beat them up for something sacrilegious they had done during service.

My later years in residential school, from 1957 to 1959, were more fruitful because of our involvement in track and field with Reverend Miller. When he arrived at Old Sun, he started training us in track and field. We got so good that the other residential schools in the Treaty 7 area refused to run against us. So we had to run against white high schools in Calgary, Cardston, and Lethbridge, and then in a provincial high school championship in Stettler and in indoor track and field in Edmonton, Winnipeg, and Saskatoon.

There were trophies like the Treaty 7 Trophy, the Bishop Shield, the Chief and Council Shield, and the Cannon Stockton Memorial Trophy. Because nobody wanted to run against us for those trophies, they were awarded to Old Sun for good. They were displayed in the hallway leading to the chapel. Whatever happened to them, I do not know. Because we were so well trained, Randy Ayoungman won the Tom Longboat Trophy as the outstanding athlete in Canada. He won every mile race that he competed in and ran in the Commonwealth Games in Winnipeg. Unfortunately, he died relatively young.

When I left Old Sun at the end of June 1959, another school year would fast approach. I told my dad that I wanted to go back to school, but not to Old Sun. So he made arrangements for me to attend high school in Cardston and stay at St. Paul's Indian Residential School, on the Blood reserve. Until I got there, I did not realize that Bill Starr, who abused so many at Old Sun, was now the senior boys' supervisor at St. Paul's. A short time after my arrival, I was having problems passing water with a lot of pain. Of course I had to confide in him. He took me into the boys' clothing room where I had to drop my pants. He started to check my penis almost to the point of playing with me. I almost had an erection, and that's when I pulled away from him. I was taken to the local hospital to be checked. I had syphilis because I had had sex with a girl before I left for St. Paul's.

He used to take me and other senior boys to Lethbridge to watch a movie. He would buy a bottle of whiskey, and we all drank. At times he tried to touch us, but by then we were older so we fought him off. When Christmas holiday rolled around I left, never to return.

My level of learning in school was probably at a Grade 6 level, but I did not worry about it. I was busy exploring life at Siksika without the confines of Old Sun. I worked at an assortment of jobs, and I also got married. Kathy Calf Robe and I tied the knot in June 1962. We were only together for a short time, though. I left the reserve for Edmonton in August to attend an upgrading course (to Grade 9) sponsored by Indian Affairs. After I completed the course in January 1963 and returned home, I stayed only long enough until I could take a six-week survival course with the King's Own Calgary Regiment (B Squadron), which began in February.

I did not think much about my life with Kathy because I left the reserve again in August to start my first off-reserve job in Sault Ste. Marie, Ontario. Ironically, it was in a residential school called Shingwauk Hall. This was my first time being away so far from home, but I had no trouble dealing with loneliness since I went through that in Old Sun. I spent about eight months there before returning home, and, while there, I met a girl older than me who had recently come back from the United States after splitting up with her husband. I was very immature, to say the least. She knew I had problems, but she never probed me for any information. We have a boy named Dwayne, but I have never met him.

I sometimes wondered what I would be if I had not gone to residential school and had a normal upbringing. I had begun to see just how poor my education really was. What would I be if I had not suffered emotional, physical, and sexual abuse? In formal education settings, I was learning very fast that I was incompetent. I had been taught in residential school that I would never last in the real world, and, in that outside world, I faced many obstacles and uncertainty in my careers as a result of my lack of training. But because of my resilience, I overcame my low self-esteem, and I am proud of what I achieved for myself in the real world. I once had a co-worker who said to me, "You know, Art, you would have been a very powerful man if you had not attended residential school." I think her assessment of me has some merit.

When I left Siksika in 1963 to work in Sault Ste. Marie, I was twenty-one years old, and the boys I looked after were not much younger than me. I knew the system, so my adjustment was minimal. It was the same routine that I had known for ten years, but now I was on the other side. One difference, though, was that I was not a monster like those I ran into during my school time. I used to tell the boys about what I went through. They did not believe me, but it is hard to comprehend what we actually experienced. Even today, when our stories come out, they are pretty hard to believe.

My term at Shingwauk Hall ended in April 1964. I returned home, and it did not take long for Kathy and me to get back together. The result was the birth of two children, Arthur Grant, in 1965, and Kimberly, in 1966. I worked as a seasonal farmhand for Shep Hule, a local farmer, for quite some time, but, in May 1966, I decided to try something different; I became a waiter at the old Queen Hotel in Gleichen. That's when I became involved with Delphine Black Horse. Kathy and I officially split up in June. I was content to stay with Delphine, but when I received an offer in August from Shingwauk Hall to take the position of senior boys' supervisor, I accepted and left everything and everyone from Siksika behind.

As the senior boys' supervisor, I was also responsible for taking care of sports. Quite by accident, I came across the sport of judo. I used to go to the Sault Ste. Marie YMCA on a weekly basis for some fun. One day I went into the judo room and met Horst Pfaff. We talked for a while and agreed to meet again so he could teach me the basics of judo. Well, to make a long story short, I started with individual instructions from him and at the same time started a club at Shingwauk Hall. We trained at the school

and at the Y and started entering competitions locally, in North Bay, in Sudbury, in Toronto, and in Mississauga. I quickly advanced to the rank of orange belt solely on my fighting skills.

I truly enjoyed sports and supervising the boys, and I also found myself taking the role of advisor to the senior girls' supervisor. Barbara Lynn Garrett started at the same time as I did, fresh out of high school, with the goal of working as a missionary. Her bishop, the Bishop of Windsor, Ontario, was instrumental in getting her the job at Shingwauk Hall. She came from a very sheltered, well-to-do family in Essex, Ontario, not far from Windsor. This was her first time away from her family. She was in many ways a child who wanted to do some good by working as a missionary, but I think Shingwauk Hall was the wrong place for her. She was inexperienced about life and its harsh realities. She had no idea what she was getting into. Barb had high school boyfriends like everyone else, but no real meaningful relationships. She believed in no sex until marriage. She was saving herself for the right man. She had good solid family values.

At first she did not interest me at all. I simply looked at her as a co-worker who I had to assist many times because of her problems with the senior girls. She just could not handle them. Many times she came crying to me, and all I could do was advise her on what to do and to make sure the girls understood that she was in charge and must be respected.

Many of the male staff were after her, but she was always beside me and wanted me to take her to a show or for a pizza since we both had the same day off. My preference was to go to the bar to play shuffleboard and sip some beer, but she could not join me because she was not yet twenty-one. Every afternoon after the students had gone back to school, she would come into my room, and we would lie on the bed talking. Eventually we started making out, but it didn't go beyond that point. Of course, I wanted more. She kept me at bay for quite some time, until one night we were in her room making out as usual, and this time it went further. For the first time, we had sex. After that we became even closer.

One day she came into my room and said, "Art, I have not had my period." She was worried, but, of course, it did not bother me at all. Three days later she came running into my room after the students had gone for breakfast. She was jumping up and down in front of me yelling, "I got my period!" She grabbed me and kissed me. She was so happy, but it had absolutely no effect on me. In fact, I thought the way she was acting was pretty funny.

Just before Christmas in 1966, she came to me and said, "Art, I have spoken to my parents and have their permission to bring you home for Christmas." I protested, but in the end she won. We travelled together by bus from Sault Ste. Marie across the border into Michigan, then down to Detroit and back across the border to Windsor. For the first time in my short life, I spent Christmas with a family. In residential school, there were never any Christmas celebrations. I was in awe of the amount of work and preparation they went through to put on a one-day event. I was more or less the guest of honour, and her extended family showed up just to meet this Indian from Alberta. It was almost like a gong show, and I was the star attraction.

We traveled back to Sault Ste. Marie to get ready for New Year's and to welcome the students back from their holidays. Barb told me that she was going to quit her job at the end of January, but she stressed that she was not leaving me, and our relationship would continue until such time that she came back. She also indicated to me that she was going to talk to her parents about us. During that January, she spent every night with me. She practically moved into my room. When she did leave, I did not hear from her until March. She called me from Florida, where she'd been sent by her parents to be with her grandparents until spring. I guess after she spoke to them about us, they decided it was best to send her away to forget me, but it did not work. She kept in contact with me at least twice a week by phone. When she did return to Windsor, in April, her parents bought her a new Mustang and told her to forget about me and get on with her life. She wrote to me, and telephone calls kept us in touch.

In April of 1967, during the Easter holidays, I got a shock with a phone call from Delphine Black Horse. She was in town on leave from her job as a hostess at the Indian Pavilion at Expo 67 in Montréal. I was surprised, considering that I had officially broken up with her over Barb. Nevertheless, she was in town, and she wanted to spend time with me while she was there. I was so glad to be with her again for that entire Easter weekend that I did not feel guilty or ashamed of myself for going astray on Barb. I also travelled to Montréal in June to spend a few more days with her.

In July, Barb called and wanted me to come down to Windsor and spend some time with her. I gladly obliged. By this time she had moved out of her parents' home and was living with a friend. When I returned to work at the school, I just kept busy with work, and I looked forward to going to Saskatoon for the annual child care conference held in August. I was beginning to have feelings of uncertainty about our relationship, and during the conference, I made up my mind to break up with her after I returned.

However, when I got back from Saskatoon, I found something like twenty-odd letters from Barb in my box. I went through them and found out that her parents had kicked her out. Apparently she was given a choice: me or her family. She chose me, which made me feel very special and responsible for her. I contacted her, and we agreed that she should move to Sault Ste. Marie and I would pay her rent until she got a job. I spoke to my boss, Alan Wheatly, about her staying with me. He said the bishop would not like it very much, so that was that.

After Barb arrived, we quickly made plans to marry after my divorce from Kathy Calf Robe became final in October 1967. We had no help financially or anything. We made all the arrangements and paid for it ourselves. I contacted my dad, and he advised me on what to do after the wedding regarding Barb's acceptance into our band as a member.

December 2, 1967, was our day. We were married at a United Church by a minister of that church. Barb's sister, Carolyn, came from Toronto to stand by her as the bridesmaid, and my friend Mel Baxter was my best man. Add two witnesses—my friend's wife and my judo instructor, Horst Pfaff—and that was our big wedding. Our reception was held at Mel's apartment, and our guests were all from the YMCA judo club.

Barb talked a lot about the family she wanted, four children, two boys and two girls. I held firm that we should not start a family right away, not until we were sure our marriage was strong. She agreed but said she would bring the subject up every so often so I wouldn't forget.

On April 1, 1968, I left my job at Shingwauk Hall to attend upgrading through the Canada Employment Centre. Barb and I moved to the west end of Sault Ste. Marie, the Italian section. However, I had to leave my classes because of a severe acne infection. I had hopes of returning in the fall, but we only stayed in Sault Ste. Marie until August because Noel Goater had found me a job in Moose Factory, Ontario, near the southern end of James Bay. I had to be there right away, so Barb stayed behind to take care of financial and personal business. Two weeks later, Barb joined me on the island. We stayed for two years.

When I arrived at Moose Factory, I started a judo club there for my senior boys, but it expanded quickly to the whole island. While I was there, three black belts from Toronto came to train me, and in the fall of 1969 they promoted me from orange to green belt. Early in the New Year, one black belt and a brown belt from Petawawa came for two weeks to observe me and teach me the finer points for the test in the blue belt, which I passed. In the early spring of 1970, the Canadian amateur sports organization paid for my trip to Toronto to train with Frank Hashito, who had the sixth-degree black belt, which was the highest ranking in Canada. I successfully completed my training with him and succeeded in passing for my brown belt, the highest belt before the black belt. When I returned to the "Moose," I put on a very successful judo demonstration at the local school gym show. The entire island came out to watch. I was proud of my judokas, who put on an excellent performance. It was an honour to watch them and to see the fruits of my two years of hard work. That was my swan song. I left the island right after that, in April of 1970.

I resigned because I had decided to attend the correction staff college in Kingston, Ontario. During the six weeks training I needed to enter the correctional field, Barb stayed on the island an extra two weeks and then moved to her parents' place in Essex, where she waited for me. I joined her on every weekend leave I had. When I completed my training, I joined her and later received an offer of employment at the maximum security prison in Kingston. We talked about the offer for a long time, and her dad, Bob, advised me to accept it, for it was a good opportunity for me. Barb and I, however, decided to reject the offer. I wanted to continue with post-secondary education. I contacted Indian Affairs in Toronto and told them I wanted to attend Mount Royal College, in Calgary, to study child care. I was advised to wait for instructions.

When I finished at Kingston and moved to Essex to join Barb, she informed me that she had stopped taking her birth control pills, and she wanted a baby, for it was time. There was no arguing, and she conceived right away. Indian Affairs contacted me and told me all arrangements were completed, travel finances were in the mail, and wished me good luck. We moved to Calgary.

After I started at Mount Royal College in the fall of 1970, I used to leave Barb alone in our apartment while I went partying with friends, and I developed an ongoing sexual relationship with a fellow student. So Barb left me and headed back to Windsor to her parents. Just before Christmas, I phoned her to ask her to come back. I remember her asking, "Is this what you want?" I told her, "Yes," and she did come back to me. Why, I really don't know. She must have felt something for me. Looking back on it now, I know she really did love me; otherwise, she would have refused and stayed in the comfort of her parents' home. Like a fool, I did not recognize her feelings for me.

Our daughter, Patti, was born in March 1971, at the Holy Cross Hospital in Calgary. We ended up moving to Prince Albert, Saskatchewan, in September 1971. I got another position at a student residence, and, of course, I formed another judo club. The club, which started in early 1972, consisted of about forty participants at first, but eventually I was left with only about twelve dedicated students. We formed an alliance with the Prince Albert Judo Club, training with them on a weekly basis and joining them in competitions in Saskatoon, Swift Current, Waka, and Regina, and in the Prince Albert tournament. Many of my students won trophies and advanced in the sport through promotions. After I left, on March 31, 1973, I never heard what happened to the club.

While I enjoyed my time with the boys and the judo club, my marriage to Barb was not going well. I went after a girl who supervised some of the junior boys, and I succeeded in bedding her. My womanizing and drinking became so bad that Barb finally took our daughter, Patti, and moved back to Ontario, so ending the marriage and my relationships with both Barb and Patti.

After finishing up in Prince Albert, I returned to Siksika with no specific idea of what I wanted to do, since I was still suffering from post-separation syndrome, and I was in a lot of emotional pain. At that time, my dad, retired from Indian Affairs, sat me down and asked me what I was going to do with my life. I told him I was thinking of going back to Ontario to look for Barb and my baby, but, deep down inside of me, I knew that was futile. Still, I wanted another chance. After all, I did love her, although I was never fully aware of this until she left.

My dad said to me, "That life of yours is gone. Now you should move on and get yourself straightened around and never mind crying and tearing your guts out over something that is no longer in your control." After several more sessions with him, I decided to apply to Mount Royal College in the social sciences field. I applied to Indian Affairs and was accepted for sponsorship.

I registered at college for the 1973 fall semester, and I was put into a second-year course in applied social science, which handicapped me right away. I was not ready for school because of my mental condition. I gave it a try but could not adjust to the routine. By Christmas, I was on the verge of flunking out. My advisor told me to withdraw from all subjects except for the one in which I was getting an A. For the second semester, I was classified as a part-time student, and I took some other inconsequential subjects so that my student allowance wouldn't be discontinued.

As the term came to an end in April of 1974, I started scanning the want ads for work. I did not want to go back to the student residences. I came across an ad from the government of the Northwest Territories, which was looking for a youth development worker for the Fort Smith detention centre for juveniles. Since I was familiar with the work, I applied. I was contacted to attend an interview in Edmonton. Shortly afterwards, I was contacted by the superintendent that I was successful, and I was offered employment right after my college term ended.

I moved to Fort Smith. I did not like the place too much, but it was a job. I was informed by my supervisor that I had been recommended as an escort for students going to Vancouver for a three-week holiday. In June, we left Fort Smith for Edmonton to board the VIA Rail to Vancouver. I had only two boys to supervise, so we did a lot of things that we enjoyed without any planning. We visited Chinatown, Gastown, and the Pacific National Exhibition. I had a ball with those boys. Late in the afternoon, they used to tell me go and have beer: "Mr. Bear Chief, we will wait for you outside." At the end, we travelled back to Edmonton and then to Fort Smith.

Before the summer ended, though, I was desperate to leave Fort Smith. I started looking at want ads in the *Edmonton Journal* and came across an ad from the Alberta Human Rights Commission, which was looking for a human rights officer for the Calgary office. I applied, and much to my surprise, I was invited for an interview. I was subsequently informed by the director of the commission that I had been the runner-up but that there was an opening at their Edmonton office, "Would I be interested?" Of course I was interested, and I accepted.

I did not have very much money in my bank account, and I did not know what to do. I contacted my friend Johnny Kilcup, who was working in Saudi Arabia, and informed him of my situation. He asked for my banking information and advised me to sit back and wait for my money. Several days later, my bank called: $1,500 US had been deposited into my account by a Saudi oil company. Boy, was I surprised!

When I arrived in Edmonton, I had to look for an apartment. I found one and put a deposit on it. The manager informed me that he would hold it for 48 hours. I went to local welfare office to see whether I could get some kind of assistance. While I was speaking to the receptionist, a classmate from Mount Royal came out of his office. Well, needless to say, I was assisted with temporary lodging at a hotel and at the local YMCA, and with the first month's rent and a damage deposit. What luck! I stayed in Edmonton until the end of March and then transferred to the Calgary office on April 1, 1975.

I stayed with Alberta Human Rights Commission until October 1976 and then moved back to Edmonton to join the Public Service Commission of Canada as their regional Native employment coordinator, covering all of Alberta and the Northwest Territories. I put on a very successful Native employment conference for Treaty 7 in Calgary in January 1978. As a result, I was given a merit increment in my 1978 evaluation. Subsequent to that I was visited by the personnel manager for Northern Affairs, in Ottawa, who asked me to take on the job of coordinator of Native employment for their "North of 60" program, which was based in Ottawa.

I thought about it for a while, wondering whether I should accept this challenge. I asked my dad for some advice. Without hesitation, he told me to accept the challenge. He told me, "You are as good as anyone, and do not be afraid to ask for help when you don't know the answers, and don't forget, you may be the only Native in that office. Others who may follow you, they will be judged on your work and image." He made me see myself as a trailblazer, so I contacted the personnel manager to accept the job. He told me to sit back and wait for the paperwork to be completed and the instructions that would follow. I moved to Ottawa on April 1, 1978.

Before I left Alberta, my dad sat me down with my mother. He told me that he was going to pass his Indian name on to me, and my mother said to me, "Take the name. Your dad is giving it to you." Omahkapi'si means Big Wolf. There was no fanfare, and I never mentioned it to anyone. I am proud of this offering, and I felt so privileged to receive his name. Sad to say, my father would pass away in September 1978. I lost a trusted advisor and a father I never really got to know because of residential school. I stayed in Ottawa until September 1979, when I was seconded to Transport Canada in Edmonton.

Prior to leaving Ottawa, I was transferred to Corporate Affairs to rewrite the 1979–80 departmental Strike

Contingency Plan. I finished it before I left for my assignment in Edmonton with Transport Canada, and, much to my surprise, I was given a merit increment after my evaluation in April 1980. I was also notified by Ottawa personnel that I had been reassigned to Regina, where I stayed until April 1981. I then moved back to Ottawa, and, while I was there, I was visited by the Siksika band manager and chief, the late Leo Youngman. He asked whether I would be interested in a secondment to assist in the development of a Siksika Nation personnel policy and procedures manual.

I arrived at Siksika in August of 1981. To make this story short, let me just say that it was a disaster. Youngman lost the Siksika election in the fall of 1981, and after that I was in limbo and never actually accomplished anything. It was a waste of talent.

Early in 1982, Mother sat me down to talk about her house. She wanted to pass it to the elder members of our family, but since none of them wanted it, she asked me if I would be willing to take it over after she moved out to her trailer. On April 1, 1982, I moved in. I was scheduled to return to Ottawa in February 1983, but I decided not to go. A friend in personnel advised me to take a leave without pay for six months and think about my future.

When I first left the reserve in 1963 to work at the Shin-gwauk Hall student residence, my English wasn't very good. I noticed some of the senior boys were correcting me in some phrases of the English language, telling me, "That's not how you pronounce it. You say it this way." I thought it was fun being taught by my senior boys. Of course they made fun of me, but it was all in a good spirit. I was never offended by them because I never really thought they were important at that time of my life. I was a twenty-one-year-old boy with not too many worries about life itself. In hindsight, though, that job was my first foray into a world I knew very little about.

My ex-wife Barb used to write all my reports. I would tell her what I wanted to say, and she would just go ahead and write it. When she finished, we would go through it to make sure it was what I wanted. In 1968, in Moose Factory, I had to do a report for a psychiatrist from Toronto about one of my students who was an epileptic. In it, I simply described what I did with the student after he was transferred to my dorm. I related all of it to Barb, and she wrote the report for me. That was when Barb started to talk to me about my serious lack of understanding of both written and spoken English. She started to encourage me to return to school to upgrade myself so that I could become more proficient in the English language. Only then did it occur to me that I was incompetent in English. But it really didn't bother me too much.

When I was accepted into the correctional staff college in Kingston, Ontario, in May 1970, I was not prepared for the amount of writing that was involved in the course I was taking. When I finished my course, I was told that I was not a candidate for the probation and parole area because of my lack of writing skills but that I would be a perfect fit as a correctional officer. I was recommended for an additional twelve days of correctional officer training, which I completed. But I was hurt and insulted by being told I wasn't good enough for probation and parole work. When I spoke to Barb about it, I told her, "You watch and see. I will show them that I am just as good as anyone, if not better." I guess my Bear Chief pride and stubbornness kicked in, which is why I chose to attend Mount Royal College in Calgary in 1970 instead of accepting employment at the Kingston maximum security penitentiary.

My first real taste of report writing on my own was at Fort Smith, in 1974, after my second year at college. It was a juvenile open-custody institution, and I had to do a written report in the log book at the end of my shift. This helped me a lot to improve my writing skills. Although senior staff criticized my writing, doing these reports really did help me to improve. When it came to writing, I was never too proud to ask for assistance.

Just when I thought I had gotten my writing skills to the point where they were acceptable, I got a job with the Alberta Human Rights Commission as an investigating officer in November 1974. It got tricky during the short period of time that I was in Edmonton. I spent a lot time trying to improve my writing with a friend and co-worker by taking my reports on investigations to him for editing. I learned a lot from him, and he was very happy to assist me. When I transferred to the Calgary office in April 1975, the individual who assisted me there was a co-worker who had a degree in English. I was brought to his attention by my secretary. She didn't want to offend me by telling me that my report was not right grammatically. So my co-worker went to work on me, teaching me how to form sentences and use periods, commas, nouns, adjectives—anything to do with English correctness. I learned a lot from this gentleman, and I remain grateful for his patience and understanding. My report writing eventually got so good that my secretary never had to correct my grammar when I handed in reports for typing. She always complimented me on my improvement. She became a very good friend.

After I left Human Rights in October 1976 and moved back to Edmonton to work with the Public Service Commission of Canada, I became responsible for a brand new program. I had to build it from the ground up because my predecessor had done nothing of any substance during his short, six-month term. I did a lot of proposal writing in support of the increased participation of Native people in the public service and did a lot of writing of job descriptions for Natives. To advocate the hiring of Native individuals, I travelled to many First Nations and Métis settlements to inform them of the opportunities that existed in the Public Service Commission. This was challenging at times, and so was the stubbornness of senior managers in the government. But it was fun until the next opportunity arrived.

When I accepted the offer to transfer to Northern Affairs in Ottawa, I really did not know what I was getting into. Looking back on it now, the job really was over my head and out of my league. I found myself in a social environment I had no knowledge of. You might say I was like a fish out of water.

When I talked to my dad about the situation, he said, "Son, you made a choice. Now it's up to you to make the most of it. I do not want you to quit without at least trying to see if it will work out for you." And, as usual, he added, "You are only as good as what you want to be. Do not pretend to be somebody else. Be yourself and know your limits and do not be afraid to ask for help." With those words in my mind, I knew I would be all right. I had taken pride in working on my writing and my language skills. When I took the job with Northern Affairs, I thought I was at a level where my skills would be acceptable. But I was in for a surprise.

When I arrived in Ottawa, everything they did was totally different from what I had learned previously. I said to myself, "Here I go again. I have to learn how to do it their way, at another level." But I managed to survive the dog-eat-dog world of Ottawa bureaucracy as I made my way through the maze of learning how it's done in their world. I never really did fit into that lifestyle, though, and when my father passed away in September 1978, I was on the verge of quitting my job in Ottawa to move back West.

Instead, I decided to stick it out until something else came along. I remember one time I was asked to write a memo for the deputy minister of Northern Affairs on the subject of Native participation north of 60. I spent two days writing and rewriting until I thought it was perfect. Even my secretary thought so. However, when it was sent to the minister's office for approval, I got a shock. It was rejected. At first, I was offended and insulted, but then I said to myself, "Okay, now let's see what my supervisor is going to write. So we sat down to rewrite it in accordance with how Ottawa bureaucracy writes. When we were done, it was longer but basically said the same thing as my previous memo. I told him, "It's no different from what I wrote that they found unacceptable." He explained that this was how things were done. So I accepted it, and then I made sure that every memo I wrote went to my supervisor first before it was sent on. I may not have agreed with how they did things, but I adjusted. Gaining acceptance into the world of Ottawa bureaucracy was just like residential school. I learned by watching and following the leader, but not blindly. I was still my own person.

These challenges were a direct result of the residential school's lack of emphasis on education and instead on trying to beat the Indian out of me. However, I managed to succeed in spite of my inadequacy in the English language. It goes back to my resilience and the spirit of my ancestors. One example of my work with the federal government in Ottawa stands out in my memory. Our offices were located in Hull, and, like everything in the federal government, everything had to be bilingual. I was doing the work of advertising a position for which I had to do the recruiting. I asked the language people how long it was going to take for the posting to be translated into French. They told me, "We are behind. We cannot give you a time frame." So while mulling over what to do, I decided I was going to try the translation myself. I gathered other advertisements

59

similar to mine and spent a couple of days going over them line by line. Then I prepared my posting and passed it on to my francophone friend for editing. When he had done that, he came back to me and said, "Tell Language there are only two mistakes." I said to him with a smile on my face, "I did it myself."

"Bullshit!" he said, and took it down to the Language department to ascertain who did it. Much to his surprise, he was informed that it wasn't their work for it was not in their books as an assignment. He came back to my desk and asked, "Seriously, Art, who did it?" I explained to him what I did. He could not believe it. He walked away shaking his head. Because of my exemplary work, the Language director gave me a letter of commendation.

I often wondered what I might have been if I had been schooled properly and had graduated from high school and post-secondary education. I think my opportunities would have been endless. As I said earlier, a former co-worker told me, "Art, if you hadn't gone to residential school, you would have been a powerful man." And, years later, my friend and fellow residential school survivor, Duncan Winnipeg, now living in Saskatchewan, told me in one of our many telephone conversations, "You were always smart in school, Art." Yet in the back of my mind, I was saying, "Bullshit! I always thought I was stupid." Obviously, though, in spite of my limits, I proved to myself and many others that, as long as I performed my duties to the best of my abilities, I was as good as anyone.

My biggest obstacle was the English language, but, like everything else, I overcame it enough to succeed in white society. Nobody can ever take that away from me. No wonder my late father was so proud of me. I think all along he understood my obstacles but never said anything about them, instead always encouraging me to push forward. "Thanks, Dad, for believing in me!" It has been a lifelong journey for me to get where I am now, and in spite of my many dysfunctions, I managed to have a very successful career in the public service, a record that no one can take away from me.

If my father had still been alive, it probably would have been very different. Instead I chose to resign from the government, stay at Siksika, and take my chances. Having my mother's house had a tremendous influence on my decision to remain at Siksika. But when I went to talk to her, she told me, "Your father must be turning in his grave. He told you to never come back." For the way I was treated after I went to work for the band administration, he probably was justified in turning in his grave. "I am sorry, Dad, for not living out your dream for me."

When I began applying for new work, I had sent an application to the Fort McKay Indian Band for the position of band manager. I was successful, and so I moved to Fort McMurray in February 1983. The reserve there was very poor, with no indoor plumbing or water. I resigned after a few months, and, by May, I had moved back home.

I lived on EI until I got a job with the Siksika housing office. In September, I competed for the housing director's job. I was unsuccessful but was offered the job of maintenance supervisor. In the absence of the director, I served in his place, and, in 1986, I was asked to develop and implement a rental housing program through the Canada Mortgage and Housing Corporation. I headed this program until April 1989.

After weighing my options, I realized that I would never have a chance of being promoted to director, at least not with the senior manager in place, because in band administration, you cannot be smarter than the boss. Then you become a threat to them, are ostracized by everyone, and end up an outcast with no support. So I resigned from housing to try my luck elsewhere. I managed to get a contract with the Blackfoot Crossing Historical Society for a six-month term paid by the province. After that I was unemployed until April 1990. Then I competed successfully for the position of Siksika health director.

The program had a lot of in-house morale problems with staff. I walked into a very unstable situation. Needless to say, I ended up getting fired. It was not because of incompetence or anything to do with job performance. Some employees wrote a letter of complaint to the senior manager. They said I kept my door closed, that I intimidated people and wasn't friendly. I think they said my armpits smelled, too. So I advised the senior manager that I would stay until the end of the 1991 fiscal year and then leave. I told him I didn't want to work for a manager who doesn't support line management. He was offended by that, pulled me out of my office, and put someone else in there. He moved me to another office where I sat and did nothing. What a waste of money and manpower!

I was out of work until May 1994, when I succeeded in getting a bylaw officer job with our police service. I subsequently attended the justice college in Edmonton and successfully completed the Special Constable Training course, for which I received a certificate and regimental number. But in October 1997, I was fired. My letter stated insubordination and poor performance, although in my job evaluations for 1995 and 1996, I was classified as meeting all the requirements, and there were no documents in my file citing me for insubordination. Nevertheless, I was fired. When I appealed to the chief of police, he stated that I was fired under the police code of conduct. But the code wasn't even approved until 1998. I mean, somebody must have enough of a brain to notice the discrepancy, but who am I to dispute our learned leaders? I was unemployed until April of 1998, when I won the competition for the job in security at the Calgary office. Then I was transferred into the "Combined Effort Program" after a competition in May 2001. I lived in a basement suite in Calgary for a year or so and then moved to an apartment that served me well until August 2005, when I returned to Siksika to sit on my ass and get paid for nothing until my retirement in 2007.

I faced many hardships and obstacles in my work with our band administration, but I did the best I could to keep myself employed, never giving up looking for work when I found myself without a job. I admit that I found the long periods of time without work hard to take, and I often turned to drinking too much. Still, I remained determined to learn what I could about myself and the community and culture I had neglected for so many years.

When I returned to Siksika, I had to start all over again learning who I really was. It's like returning to a crime scene to gather all the facts and determine what is true. I tell you, it was a real struggle to accept my true self without feeling shame. Some things that I learned, though, such as renewing my Blackfoot language skills, were very satisfying.

You can probably guess that my Blackfoot speaking abilities left a lot to be desired when I moved back to Siksika. I still understood it, but the speaking part was a little difficult since my first language had been English for many years. I never forgot the language, but I did not remember how to say many words.

When I was at work, three elders used to come into my office—Joe Cat Face, Phil Many Guns, and Freddie Doore, all of whom passed on some time ago. They used to instruct me. First they would tell me to shut the door and lock it. Then they would sit and begin to talk about any subject totally in Blackfoot, with no English. When they pointed at me, I would have to respond in Blackfoot. If I switched to English, Old Joe would wave his finger and say in Blackfoot, "Speak Blackfoot." They all laughed when I could not pronounce certain words and corrected me on how to say them. These elders never criticized me for not knowing the correct pronunciation, but instead they joked about how I was struggling with their teaching, I learned a lot from them, and what they taught me can never be found in books.

Their teaching came from their hearts and their sincerity. Needless to say, I picked up our language very quickly. Their teaching was invaluable to me in the beginning of my reintegration into our culture. I will value their teaching and friendship forever. I miss those old guys. They taught me the patience of our grandparents and the gentle nature of our ways. There were no harsh words. When I made a mistake, there were smiles on their faces, and they encouraged me not to give up. I treasure those few moments, and I am proud that one of our current elders, who used to be on the Siksika council, came to me and said, "You know, Art, I was really proud of you, speaking our language like you have never been away." He then made references to our younger generation who don't speak our language.

I reclaimed my mother tongue and felt pride; Old Sun Indian Residential School had failed to destroy my first language! For that I am happy, but my residential school experience did cause me to stay away from traditional cultural practices. I envy those who turned back to our Blackfoot culture and practice it with honour and pride.

Maybe I cannot turn back into our traditional practices because, over the years, I forgot so much. Beginning with my time at Shingwauk Hall, I had a lot of white friends who I used to socialize with in the local hotels. I remember an incident at a bar in Sault Ste. Marie when an Indian came and got drunk, and everybody was making fun of him. I accepted it. But they made a point of saying to me, "You're different, Art. You are not like that." The drunken Indian was thrown out very unceremoniously, and everybody was having a good laugh over it. In the same hotel bar sometime after that, a white man who was very drunk was sitting on a chair. When he fell off the chair, everybody started laughing, saying that he was just having a good time. The bartender picked him up off the floor and placed him back on his chair.

You might say that, in those times, I was an "apple Indian," red on the outside and white on the inside. I went along with the ridiculing of Indians, including my own criticisms of them, and laughing at them. Residential school made me ashamed of being an Indian, and, in my case, Old Sun was very successful in making me deny who I was. I was confused and mixed up as to who I really was.

In many of the places where I worked, I was the only Indian, and when colleagues talked about Indians, it was the same old scenario: "You are not like them, Art. You are different." How was I different? Because I chose to hide the fact I am Indian? The bottom line was that I was ashamed of being Indian. I wanted to be part of white society and to be one of them. Only one thing stood in my way—I was an Indian. Acceptance on their part was because I was a co-worker. They had to take the Indian begrudgingly, as part of me. I was ashamed of my Blackfoot language and would never speak it in public. After all, in residential school we were punished for speaking it, and I mean severely.

When I was working off reserve, I was ashamed of who I am, and I turned away from our culture, desperately trying to be accepted into white society. I was successful in turning my back on my culture because I functioned very well in mainstream society. I had very few friends who were Indians, and the ones I associated with were professionals like me. We thought alike. Most of my girlfriends were white or Métis who never wanted to have much to do with Indians. I accepted this with no guilt or shame. If you want to know the truth, I was very content and happy. I was a perfect "apple Indian."

Deep inside of me, though, there was a restless spirit that wanted to come out and return to our ways, but I kept it at bay because I was quite happy with who I thought I was and content with my life and career and all the benefits that came with it. It never occurred to me to look at myself in the mirror to see who I really was. That was of no concern to me. I thought I was happy, but really, deep inside of me, turmoil was going on, like good and evil fighting for my soul. I always said, "What have the Indians done for me lately? Why should I have to stand up for them? Why can't they be like me?" I really was a mixed-up individual who enjoyed the luxury of white society.

One piece of the puzzle makes me ask, "How could I have been so naïve?" I thought having a white girlfriend was equivalent to acceptance in white society. How stupid of me! There were so many Native girls I turned my back on. Did I think that marrying a white girl in 1967 was going to bring me prestige? I really don't know—maybe. I never did think of it as being classy, but it was kind of unusual for an Indian to be married to a white girl back then.

In any event, I had forgotten so much that, when I first started staying with my current wife, I was amazed at the things she did. Take beading, for instance. I was lying on the couch one evening while she was beading. I was fascinated by that. I finally went to her and asked what she was doing. She said, "Beading, don't you know that?" I said, "No, I was not raised with that." Yet I was. I knew what beading was before I went to Old Sun. That was just one of the things I had forgotten because it was not in evidence at residential school.

The first time I met my wife Marie was after I returned from Fort McKay in May 1983 to settle down in my parental home. I went to the Calgary Stampede with a bunch of people from the reserve. We were in the Chuckwagon Bar at the Grandstand for a few drinks. I noticed a lady walk in with a white gentleman. She had a slim, well-built body and the most beautiful ass I had seen in a long time, and I had seen a lot in my travels. I asked my companions who she was. One of my female friends piped up with her name, Marie Breaker, and another said, "She's not for you, Art." Another noted that she was not a one-night stand. I went back to my drinking, thinking that she was probably involved with someone and that I would never see her again.

Much to my surprise, she walked into my office at the housing program in April 1984 and requested some leftover paints that could be donated to paint her offices. I don't remember how we started going out, but I do remember that we once went to Calgary to see Charlie Pride at the Jubilee Auditorium, and another time she showed up at my house to let me know she was going to Medicine Hat for a conference. The next thing I knew I was packing so I could go with her. In early December, we went to Calgary together, and when Marie was at a Stampede Indian Village meeting, I went to a jewelry store in the Stephen Avenue mall to buy her an engagement ring, with no idea if she was going to accept. I picked her up, and we went for something to eat. I presented the ring to her, and much to my surprise, she accepted it.

I spent Christmas at her house and asked her whether she would move in with me. She said, "I come with a package. If you don't want my excess, then I don't want you." Marie's package was her children. I accepted her condition, fully confident that her children would eventually move out to be on their own. I did not recognize then her strong bond to keeping them at home, so Marie and family moved in with me in January 1985. The first years of our relationship were very rocky, and a lot of people were dead set against us being together. We had many trials and made lots of mistakes, but for some strange reason, we always managed to overcome them.

At Easter in 1987, Marie and I traveled to Las Vegas. We were having breakfast on Good Friday, and, out of the blue, I said, "Let's get married." We talked for a while and decided to go ahead with it. Of course we had no idea what to do, so we asked our waitress. She was so happy to help us and told us, "Get a cab and tell the driver you want to get married. He will do everything for you."

Our driver first took us to the Nevada registrar to get our license. Boy, what a lineup! Young, middle-aged, and elderly couples all wanting to get married—it was something! After that was completed, our driver drove us around to various chapels so we could pick the one we wanted. We settled on the Silver Bells Chapel. We entered the chapel and told the owners we were there to get married. The first thing they said was that we needed this and that and that, and it would cost us this much. We decided to go ahead without renting too much, just Marie's flowers, and of course paying for the minister and the pictures taken. Needless to say, they wanted to supply us with a best man and bridesmaid for a price, and they told us we had to have at least one witness. Rather than paying the chapel, I asked our taxi driver if he would stand up for us. He was happy to do it, and because we refused to rent a suit for him, our main man came in wearing his coveralls, a bit dirty, but we were fine with it. When we returned home, we had our marriage blessed by the Anglican Church and hosted a reception.

We continued on with our lives of ups and downs, and Marie would leave every year for a week or two. I was not sure why, but it became a ritual for her. She always came back eventually, and we just settled back into our routine. I was starting to learn about her ways of being, and my journey home was beginning to take shape.

One of the first things I noticed about Marie was that she was always barking orders to her boys to get things going, like clean-up. Everyone had a duty to perform, including me. It was like she was in the army, ordering everybody around, so I decided to call her RSM—regimental sergeant major. The RSM is the one who puts everything in order on the parade square, and when everything is just right, he orders all the officers to march onto the parade square to take their places. Then he turns the parade over to the commanding officer and retires to the back, job completed.

We wanted to have kids of our own, but that was not possible. We settled on adopting my granddaughter Trina, and Marie had my cousin Dorothy babysitting for us while we were at work. It was a perfect arrangement because our sitter loved her like her own. Then one time, when I was in Edmonton for work, Marie showed up at my hotel. She told me that she had bad news. My daughter's family had decided to take the child back with no warning and no reason. They simply went to our sitter's house to remove her. When Marie went to pick her up after work, she was already gone, and Dorothy was so upset, she was crying.

Marie was crushed and hurt. We decided not to fight and to leave it. We were both very disappointed, but we accepted our fate. My daughter's action was very mean. It was not a matter of us being unfit or abusive; it was my ex-wife saying to both of us, "You will not be happy!" She had finally taken her ultimate revenge against me.

Marie's love for her children is, without question, very intense and protective. She wanted them close by, and she ruled their lives. She was the same with her whole family:

mistreat them, and you have a fight with a pit bull on your hands. She might not have teeth like a pit bull, but her words will cut you to pieces. I know: I have been subjected to them.

As the years went by, her boys were always living with us. It became a sore point for me because I believe that children should eventually leave the nest and go out on their own to chart their own paths. Marie would rather have them living at home until the day they die. This eventually led to my demand that they get their own place. She was not pleased about this, so she moved out with them to a rental house next to her daughter's home. She called me to say that she was going to work on settling them in their new house, and when that was all done, she would move back to our house. I did not think that grown adults needed to be held by the hand and shown how to live on their own, but that was her way.

Our marriage has now passed the twenty-five-year mark, and we still disagree over her children. I guess that will never change, but I am grateful for all that Marie has taught me about parenting and family and for influencing me to become a more responsive and loving person, especially with her grandchildren. Marshall, for example, lived with us for two or three years, and then he continued to stay with us quite a bit. Marshall is like my "true son," and several years later, with little Eva, I felt that unconditional love again. With the grandchildren, Marie was able to teach me that I could show affection through hugging and touching without fear that I was being inappropriate.

Marie has tremendous love and compassion for everyone around her, and we are still together because she understands where I am coming from. During my hiatus from work in the early 1990s, I drank a lot and caused many problems between us. I decided in 1992 to enter the St. Paul Treatment Centre, on the Blood reserve, which helped me to better understand myself. Even though Marie has to live with my alcoholism and dysfunctions, she continues to help me, and I feel a sense of belonging. Because of Marie, today I have grandchildren who really care about me. Marie is really something special!

I think I have found my home, and perhaps that is why when Patti, my daughter with Barb, called me on the phone with her mother's blessing in 1998, I was happy to hear from her. When her mother left me in 1972, Patti was only a year old, and Barb did not want me to have any contact with her. We now communicate with each other by writing and through email. She has sent me a bunch of pictures of herself and my granddaughter, which I proudly show off to visitors. I hope that one day we can see each other in person. That would make my healing of past wounds easier to bear.

When I finally came forward in 1999 to file a complaint with the Merchant Law Group against the federal government for the abuse I suffered at Old Sun, I did so with a lot of apprehension. Not knowing what to expect, right from the beginning I said to myself, "This is not about money but for my own peace of mind, and for my late friend Nelson Wolf Leg." Many years ago, on those terrible nights when we were both going through sexual abuse from our supervisor Bill Starr, we made a promise to each other to never say anything about what happened to anyone, not even our parents. We also made a pact that if one of us died, the other would come forward and talk about our abuse. I can still vividly remember Nelson, both of us lying in my bed crying and holding onto each other for protection, and scared out of our wits that Starr was going to come again. I was younger than Nelson, and I can remember him wiping the tears from my face and saying, "Keep quiet."

As I recall these incidents, I am sitting here writing and crying for all those hurts I went through as a young boy. It seems like it was only yesterday when the assaults occurred, and no matter how hard I try, they never go away. I get emotional and cry for myself, even though all those years long ago I was taught by the older boys not to cry because it showed weakness. Now, some sixty years later, I am able to release my emotions without fear of showing weakness to others, although I prefer to cry when I am alone so no one can see me. That's why I cry when I am all alone and my mind drifts back to Old Sun. My tears flow freely without fear of backlash or shame.

My abuses sat dormant inside of me all those years, and I never really thought too much about them. I guess in a sense I suppressed them in my head, and that's why they never came out of me. When I filed my papers and had to tell my story, it was very painful to go back to those times so long ago that I had tried to forget. But nevertheless, I had to revisit my time at Old Sun Indian Residential School.

In 2002, my first lawyer, Tom Stepper, suggested in many of our conversations that I really should begin counselling for my residential school abuse. Reluctantly I agreed, and since I knew of no therapists, he suggested Donna Gould. I called her, and we began meeting after Health and Welfare said it would support five sessions at a maximum of $75 per visit. This meant that I had to provide another $25 above their maximum, which was well worth the cost. Donna helped me a great deal to begin understanding what had happened to me and why I had problems. The letter she wrote for the lawyers involved in my case says a lot about what she learned about me in our sessions.

In October 2002, I was scheduled for my examination for discovery. My lawyers did nothing to prepare me for what I was about to go through. The only thing they said to me was, "Be yourself and tell the truth to best of your recollection and ability." When the day finally came, I thought I could handle it. I thought I was a tough man. Boy, was I in for rude awakening! My first day lasted about six hours.

The federal government lawyer cross-examined me and challenged every statement I made. Throughout the day I broke down crying because of the pain of remembering my sexual abuse. I literally went back to that time and place. I had to explain every single detail of my sexual abuse, including when Bill Starr tried to enter me from my asshole. This I had to say to a woman I had never met before in my life. It never entered my mind what I would have to say. Because of my emotional state and being embarrassed, we broke up the sessions so I could get my composure. There were no support services where I could go for comfort and a few kind words to ease my pain. I was left to the dogs, and, just like in residential school, I had to suck up the pain and continue on.

I was embarrassed and degraded, for I had to tell a total stranger about my sexual abuse. It had been my personal secret all those years, and now I had to share it with a stranger. I was sickened by the whole process. When it finally ended six hours later, I went home feeling numb and very much violated by the proceedings. I opened a can of Coors Light, lay down in my bed, grabbed my other pillow to hold, and began to cry softly. My memory drifted back to those times at residential school when I ran out to the field so I could cry for my mother to help me. But, just like in residential school, she never came, and, as usual, I had to deal with it by myself. I must have drifted off to sleep and did not wake up until seven the next morning, my beer still lying beside my bed. I had not even touched it. I knew my next session was coming, and I would have to go through the same hell again.

I arrived at the lawyer's office at nine for another round of cross examination from the government lawyer. Much to my surprise, she wanted to go back to some of my state-ments for clarifications and a few more questions. I told the lawyer that I was emotionally drained and not sure if I could go through another day like we did the day before.

She said she understood and would go easy on me and not push me over the limit. It was short and easy for me. At lunchtime, she advised my lawyers that she was finished, but she reserved the right for another session if needed.

My lawyer talked to me before I left and advised me that I should have someone with me. He was a little concerned about my state of mind. I told him not to worry too much about me and that my best friend Coors Light was going to be my confidante and companion to ease my pain. Before I got home, I bought some beer for dealing with my problems. When I got home, I locked my door, shut my cell phone off, opened my beer, and sat down on the floor. My mind drifted back to Old Sun. It was like a flashback, so natural and normal that I started to cry as each event passed before my eyes like on a TV screen. You don't want to think about them, but they come just the same. I cursed and swore at myself and the world and the system that sent me to that horrible place as a very young boy. I finally succumbed to the beer and drifted off into oblivion. If someone had handed me a gun at that time, I definitely would have blown my brains out. They would have saved themselves some money on my settlement.

The next day when I woke up, I was hungover, and all the pain of what I went through came back. The cycle had begun again. I did not have the opportunity to spend any time with someone who would listen to my grief. I said to myself, "But I am a survivor of residential school, so why should it be any different now? I'm so used to sucking it up and moving on." I had to attend another examination for discovery session in February 2003. Thankfully, the

caused by my experiences at Old Sun would "eventually heal" and that I would find "peace, fulfillment and enjoyment" in my future.

Another letter followed, from the deputy minister of Indian Residential Schools Resolution Canada on behalf of the Honourable Jim Prentice and the Government of Canada. He likewise expressed the government's "sincere and deep regret for all the pain that you and your family have suffered as a result of your attendance at Old Sun." He said that he recognized the burden that I had carried for many years and wished to emphasize that what I experienced was not my fault and should never have happened. He ended his apology by saying that I had shown "considerable courage and dignity" in coming forward to talk about "extremely personal and painful experiences" and that he hoped the recounting would give me "a measure of comfort," enough to allow me and my family to move forward with our lives.

Well, what about the courage it took to survive residential school—to say nothing of life itself? The apologies sounded hollow. I lost my childhood at Old Sun, and now I was supposed to get over it and move forward, as if nothing had ever happened? I wish they could walk a mile in my shoes and actually experience what I did.

My life was severely altered by my experiences at Old Sun. The emotional, mental, physical, and sexual abuse I suffered affected me deeply. It led to my self-destruction with alcohol and my many emotional dysfunctions, which resulted in failed marriages and relationships and my estrangement from my own children. It has taken me almost a lifetime to begin to come to grips with the damage it did and the toll it has taken. Old Sun Indian Residential School made me an angry, uncaring, cold individual who lacked human compassion. My anger has been with me ever since I left Old Sun in 1960, eating away at me from inside. There was very little in either of these apologies to indicate any genuine sincerity on the part of the offending agencies or any real understanding of the suffering I went through. The apologies are worth no more than the paper they are written on. Government policies damaged me before I even had a chance to start out in life. The residential school system set me up to fail, but through a combination of resilience and stubborn pride, I managed to overcome the damage enough to become relatively successful in my career. And, late in life, I was given a second chance to have the family I was never able to have before. Yes, I am very bitter and angry because of what I experienced in residential school and the fact that no one will ever be punished for what they did to me and other students at Old Sun Indian Residential School. Your apologies are of little comfort to me and probably many other survivors as well.

Speaking out about my abuses during the examination for discovery sessions was so painful, but it caused me to begin analyzing myself. I had never made any connections between the way I was treated and my behaviour towards others. The professional counselling from Donna Gould helped me greatly in dealing with myself and coming to terms with a dysfunctional personality that was no fault of my own. I have tried very hard to change, but when you have deeply rooted problems because of the traumas experienced in residential school, you don't know if you can ever recover enough to be considered a normal person. I am not a psychologist, nor do I have a degree in any kind of social work field, but from what I understand of human nature and from reading books, I will carry these scars for the rest of my life. I may look normal on the surface, but, inside, the traumas will continue to poke their heads out to let me know they are still around.

I sometimes sit and think about my residential school experiences, which never fail to bring tears to my eyes. I get so angry that I want to lash out at someone to bring me some relief to my pain and anguish. These are the times when suicide comes into my mind, and I think, "If I ended it all here today, the pain and anguish would cease to exist. I would be free from suffering."

One experience that stands out was when I worked as a bylaw enforcement officer. I carried a shotgun in my service vehicle, and one day after returning to work from a four-day weekend leave, I was pretty hungover. I proceeded to the Sand Hills area of our reserve for routine patrol. I was depressed and miserable. I stopped the vehicle and just sat there, and then, all of a sudden, I started to cry. I unlocked my shotgun, which was always loaded, put it beside me, and as I fiddled with it, I said to myself, "This is the traditional burial ground of my ancestors. What an appropriate place to take my own life." As I sat there contemplating my final move, I felt nothing, not scared, sort of like I was in a trance. Then the flashbacks began. For some unknown reason, I fell asleep. What woke me up was the operator on the radio, calling me and wanting to know my location. That was closest I ever came to committing suicide.

Although the thoughts of suicide have diminished in recent years, and I am no longer afraid of hurting myself, they still scare me. And I ask myself, "What if something triggered the demons to come out in full force and take control of me and push me to the limit?" Fortunately, through counselling and my own efforts to deal with what happened, I have come to a point where it hardly becomes serious anymore. It is just there.

It has often been said that residential school survivors have to heal or begin to heal from their abuses. I read the book *The Grieving Indian*, by Arthur H., where a Dr. Freese writes about the unresolved grief process, and I quote: "When the work of mourning isn't done, when there is unfinished business left hanging, when the grief work isn't carried to completion, then the bereaved person is left with many problems to surface in a variety of ways and to affect his life seriously." Addictions such as alcoholism and drug abuse are common with people who have not gone through the grieving process to its end. There are other effects, but these two are the most common in our Native communities.

In my opinion, many of us survivors are still in denial about what happened to us. We have not begun the grieving process, and we cannot seem to associate our dysfunctions with the abuses we suffered. If individual survivors could step forward to talk freely about what happened to them personally, it would be their first step towards their journey of healing and recovery. Until then, our personal problems will continue to affect our lives in many different ways.

I realized during my marriage to Barb that my sexual abuse caused me to have some rather strange ideas about sexuality. I masturbated a lot because I thought it was normal. I did not know why I did it, but it seemed so natural because of what I had to do to Bill Starr. I remember that one day Barb walked in on me masturbating in our bedroom. She was very upset and hurt that I would prefer to do that instead of having sex with her. But, to me, I thought it was normal. She asked why. I told her, "I don't know, but it seems the natural thing to do." She made a point of explaining to me that if I had the urge, I was supposed to go to her for relief.

I did not know how to gently caress or neck with my partner to the point where she would be ready for me. I had to be taught the finer points of lovemaking. My way consisted of crawling on top and going through the motions until I came and rolled over away from my partner because it was dirty. These are the types of abnormal behaviour that I was gradually able to change over a period of years through numerous relationships. But you must try to understand that having been sexually abused, I saw sex as dirty.

If you were sexually abused like I was, and you were ashamed of what happened to you, the end result would be denial and silence. I suffered alone, and I was always afraid of the dark because I associated the dark with sexual abuse by Bill Starr. I had nightmares well into my forties, but eventually they began to go away.

My ex-wife Barb witnessed one such nightmare I had when we lived in Moose Factory. I was on the floor in our bedroom curled into a fetal position crying and begging not to be hurt. She told me about it when I finally awoke. She was holding me and crying, asking me what was happening. I told her, "I don't know—just a bad dream. Let's go back to bed." She held onto me, stroking my hair and crying because she could not understand. I fell asleep in her arms, never knowing from the past that such tenderness was possible from another human being. I never knew up to that point in my life that I needed such tender loving care from another person. She was there, willing to provide it, but because of my abuse, I could not trust her or allow her to be my safety net. Partially because of this, our marriage failed.

For many years, I locked away in my mind all those terrible nights long ago in the hopes that they would go away. The nightmares might have become less frequent, but the abuse remained an obstacle in my journey of healing and recovery until I started to talk about it openly. Then my emotional and mental well-being began to improve. The problem of alcoholism is still an issue with me, but someday I hope to contain it.

So is the anger. Anger was something that I came out with because of everything I had been denied. This anger stayed with me. You must understand that we had no one to turn to in residential school. We were forced to watch beatings that we could not do anything about. You silently cried for that person inside of you, but you could not reach out to comfort him because you had been trained that this was a normal way of doing things. When it was over, the group simply broke up, and we went on about our business. You didn't even approach the person who got it. You avoided him, and everyone was very quiet, not saying even one word. I go back to those times now, and I still cannot understand how we could have been treated like animals with no feelings.

I think many of us left the residential schools with a lot of anger, and unresolved anger can lead to many other problems. I did not understand the many other problems associated with this anger until I started counselling. Only then did I start to make the connections between my abuse and my feelings.

As I went through life, I heard many comments about myself that were not complimentary. I heard them from people who were friends, both male and female, and of course I was offended to be told, "You are a son of a bitch and an asshole, Art. You should grow up and take responsibility for your life and be more open." Naturally, I got upset about these assessments, but still I could not reach the point of comprehending the true meaning of their words. It was like I was a child in a man's body. If I had understood, I believe I would have sought help much earlier in life.

Another of my demons from residential school is lack of compassion. I was once told that I had no compassion, but when you look at the way I was treated at Old Sun, anyone with common sense would understand why. Perhaps when I was very young, before I entered Old Sun Residential School, I understood what compassion was, but when you are that young, these things do not seem important. Growing up in residential school, I had no experience of compassion—it was unheard of. My own lack of compassion, my insensitivity, and my tendency to criticize others were all learned from the way I was treated at residential school. When I finally left Old Sun, they were a part of me, and I just assumed, or perhaps I should say believed, that callousness was a natural way of treating people. To put it simply, I was a very cold individual. You might say I was like a soldier who's been trained to suck it up and move on and not cry.

My lack of empathy extended even to people I cared about. In late 1971, in Prince Albert, before Barb and I separated, we were experiencing a lot of marital problems because of my womanizing and drinking. One night when we were having sex, she was holding onto me, and I remember her saying, "Oh Art, if only you loved me." I could not even respond to her with any gentle words. Instead, when I finished, I rolled over and did absolutely nothing to comfort her while she lay beside me crying. My feelings were zilch—no emotions. I just lay there, not making a sound until finally she fell asleep. This is what residential school did to me: I was a monster devoid of human feelings. How could I be so cruel to the woman I professed to love? I could not even reach out to her to hold her and say, "I am sorry." She did not deserve that.

I think my coldness was related to my inability to trust. When I entered residential school, I was forced to endure and also witness a great deal of physical violence. I lived in constant fear, and it eventually eroded my trust of adults. I created a wall around me so that no one could touch me.

I was unable to trust or start meaningful relationships of any kind. I did not easily make friends. I was aloof and distant from people until I knew that I could trust them. Only then would I open up to them. Once I achieved this, they became good friends, but that's the reason why I have very few friends. I chose to stay within my security wall because it gave me a sense of being safe—no one could hurt me. When I told my therapist about it, she said it was no surprise to her. Most abused children withdraw into themselves for protection. She told me that I had to learn to trust all over again and that it was going to be a difficult learning process.

With Marie's help, I am learning. The grandchildren have successfully breached my safety wall. This allows me to be more open and more of a person with feelings. As Marie put it, "Art, you had a wall around you that was so thick you would not allow anyone to come near you, but I chip away at it and have managed to break through it. You are no longer a total isolationist." She is doing a good job, for I now show love towards my grandchildren without any hesitation. I know that they have bonded with me, and I felt truly blessed when my new great-grandson came to visit me for the first time. I held him close to me, so soft and sweet. I almost cried because I never knew this could be possible for me because of my coldness and my uncaring, unloving feeling towards other people.

Perhaps this is the place where I should talk about my lack of connection with my biological children and my lack of experience as a parent. It's something I am not proud of, but I make no apologies for the way I turned out because my therapist assured me that it was not my fault. Because residential school deprived me of a relationship with my parents, the only type of parental teaching I received was of the institutional type at its worst.

When I worked at the student residences in Sault Ste. Marie, Moose Factory, and Prince Albert, I took great pride in the fact that I never once had to physically fight any boy that was under my care. Neither did I ever once try to abuse any individual physically or sexually. I was never suspended or reprimanded verbally or in writing by my superiors. My boys' care and safety came first, and I ensured that their stay was as comfortable and happy as it could be while they were away from their parents. After all, I was the substitute parent, and I had to be there for them. In the institutional setting, I knew what had been missing for me, and I could understand the meaning of responsibility, but this did not extend into the outside world.

My biological children grew up not knowing me, and I made no attempt to have any kind of relationship with them. I find it sad now that my children at Siksika won't have anything to do with me, but like so many things, it really doesn't bother me all that much. I do wish I could have been more of a father to them, but then again, because of what residential school did to me, would it really have helped? I know they are my children, but I have no feelings of closeness or the sense of bonding that is created at birth. I was not around for their births, and perhaps it is better that they did not have to grow up with the problems I had acquired from being at Old Sun.

It is true that children learn from their parents by watching and being taught by them. I did not have that luxury, and my father and I were denied that very special bonding that is supposed to happen in the formative years. I am angry and bitter about this denial of a fundamental right given to other fathers and sons. In *My Heart Soars*, Chief Dan George says, "The wisdom and eloquence of my father I passed on to my children, so they too acquired faith, courage, generosity, understanding, and knowledge in the proper way of living." But I could not pass on to my children what my father never had a chance to teach me. Instead they got an uncaring individual who never had anything to do with them. They did not deserve that. I wish I could turn the clock back and undo the residential school legacy and be given a second chance at parenting.

When my time at Old Sun was over, my family home had changed location, and I felt that I did not know my parents any more. I did not know my brothers and sisters who were born after I entered residential school. To this day, our relationship is more cordial and formal than that of siblings. How sad that they do not even know what I went through. I hope one day they will read this story.

I sometimes wonder whether I felt rejected by being sent to residential school. I don't remember feeling that way, although I always thought about why our parents never really outright fought to keep us home. But we only had two schools, a Roman Catholic and an Anglican, and they were both residential schools, so I guess there was no choice. Still, why couldn't they have just been day schools? Even if my parents didn't have an option, the government did.

I bonded with my father after his retirement, and he gave me counselling on the challenges that I had in life and my work away from Siksika. My mother was always present, and I stayed in touch with her. After all, she gave me the house after I returned home. Still, I saw Mother as a person who gave me tenderness and love before I went to Old Sun. After that, the bond that existed before was gone, lost forever. What happened to me during those ten years of separation prevented me from being an expressive, loving son.

I believe that because of all the losses I suffered, I was always looking for a mother figure in the women I had relationships with, and that is probably one reason why so many of my relationships did not last very long. I remember attending a conference on women when I was working in Edmonton in 1977. There was a dance one evening, and when I was looking for someone I might hook up with, I noticed a woman, older but with very beautiful natural looks. I asked her for a dance, and before the end of the evening, I invited her to my apartment, an invitation she graciously accepted.

When we got to my place, she took over and told me to get undressed and ready for bed. Since I was quite drunk, when she got into bed, she held me and said to me in a very gentle voice, "Go to sleep. You've had a lot to drink." When we woke up the next morning, she asked me, "Why were you crying?" I replied, "I don't know." Then she told me, "You were saying something in your language. I did not understand so I just grabbed you, held you close to me, and gently kissed your forehead, and you went back to sleep again." Before she went to the airport, she told me, "You have a lot of problems inside of you. I hope you will heal and find yourself someday."

I wanted to spend more time with her because I wanted to be close to her. Why, I don't really know. I just knew that I wanted her so that someone would hold me if I needed more TLC, but she had to get home because of commitments. I'm sure I was drawn to her because she represented a mother figure to me and, most important, someone who understood what was happening inside of me. I told her I wanted to see her again, even if I had to go to her place. In her gentle voice, she said, "No, you are young. You need someone your own age to be with. I am flattered that you want to be with me, but it's not right." She walked out, and I never saw or heard from her again. What a beautiful woman she was!

Maybe that's why, after Barb left, I stayed single for almost fourteen years. I think I was looking for some girl who might be able to give me that motherly love I wanted so bad. I was sad for myself, and even now when I see so many actions by Marie that remind of my mother, I become very angry at being denied the right to interact with my mother for that ten-year period. I wonder sometimes if Mother ever missed those times before residential school. I am sorry that I was unable to resume that relationship with her, and I am also deeply saddened by the fact that I cannot remember if I ever hugged my mother again.

Of all my brothers and sisters, I am closest with my sister Donna, and we talk quite a bit about our residential school experiences. One time, when we were talking on the phone, she was drinking and crying like so many of us do, and she said, "You know, Art, I cannot get my virginity and so much of what I lost in residential school back, so I drink to ease the pain and forget." I interrupted her by saying, "But it all comes back when we sober up." She agreed and said, "At least you forget for a while, and the pain is not there." I encouraged her to seek help by going through therapy. I cried silently for my sister while she talked on about herself. I felt ill and helpless that I could not help her to ease the pain, and, at the same time, I felt her pain inside of me and understood exactly what she was going through.

I am much closer to my older siblings than the younger ones, and I get along just fine with them. I think the younger ones are close to each other because they were together with our parents more than those of us who were placed in Old Sun, and even if they did have to go to residential school, they were allowed to go home every weekend. In my opinion, the younger ones are apprehensive about us older siblings because they did not know us. It's like we are strangers meeting for the first time, not really sure of each other's intentions. I am sorry to say that this is true. Of course, we talk to each other whenever we run into each other, at least if we are on speaking terms and not feuding about something. I find it comical and somewhat idiotic that we get into such trivial fights, but that is the way it is.

When our mother died in 2000, instead of coming together as we should have, we were torn apart because of religion. One part of the family, who are born-again Christians, and us older members, who are either Anglican or Catholic, wanted to have a traditional Catholic funeral, but the younger ones rebelled, and the fiasco that followed was, to say the least, extremely painful for me. I was hurt and humiliated by their total lack of respect for our oldest family member, who should have been the one to plan our mother's farewell, and I was incensed by their total lack of respect for the memory of our mother, who in life was gracious and dignified. I remember visiting Mother at the elders' lodge before she passed away. She said to me, "You are going to fight over my death because of religion. Just remember that."

The lack of cooperation in planning the funeral tore us apart, and it is still very much visible today. I do get along with my older brothers and one younger brother, and with Donna; we talk often and support each other in whatever way we can. However, I believe it's going to take much fence building and reconciliation to get over that shameful display of arrogance and disrespect.

While it is not that unusual for family members to disagree on matters of religion or for individuals to think differently about God and spirituality, I sometimes wonder why God put so much grief and hurt on us residential school survivors and what his purpose was. I turned away from the church when I left school, although when I worked in the student residences, I still had to go to church every Sunday. But for me then, it was only duty.

There was, however, always a light inside of me that never went out. For that reason, I always knew there was a God, but I blamed him for what happened to us, so church was not important in my life. My ex-wife Barb was religious, and a lot of it rubbed off on me. When we parted after four years of marriage, I naturally blamed God again, especially after all my prayers for her to come back were not answered. Later, I almost became an agnostic, mostly influenced by a girl I met while I was working in Ottawa. She was quite persuasive, and I thank God now that I did not succumb to her way of thinking.

Just as I was influenced by Barb's religious beliefs, so, too, did Marie's strong Catholic faith come to play a role in my life. I have gone to many different religious retreats. In the late 1980s, I attended a Kainai cursillo at Moses Lake, and, in the 1990s, I went on pilgrimages to Lac St. Anne and to Guadalupe, Mexico. I have also been to a retreat at Cochrane and a weekend retreat at Red Lake with Alcoholics Anonymous. Of course, all have been a great help for my soul and in learning to look at myself in the light of our Father in heaven.

Residential school left me in a messed-up state, and, as I have said before, I was as cold as a cucumber. I did come to learn and be positively influenced by some of the women who wanted to get to know me, but I am also very aware that I caused many of them a lot of grief and pain. To give but one example: a woman I met in Edmonton just before I left for Ottawa came to meet me at my hotel when I was there on a work trip. We did the usual thing. After we had finished, my phone rang. Lo and behold, it was a call from another woman I had dated casually while I was working in Edmonton. She wanted to see me again. As soon as I hung up the phone, I told my lady friend to get dressed and leave because I had someone else coming. She began crying and asked me how I could do something like that without any feelings or emotions. Before she left, she said she was not mad at me but that she felt sorry for me. That was the kind of person I was—selfish and cruel.

Relationships were just something I wanted with no strings attached. So many relationships simply went by, sort of like getting another notch in my gun handle. I was never sorry for my actions. I had no idea what kind of uncaring individual I was. I hurt so many women, but that never bothered me. I guess you could say I was a prime example of an asshole, simply taking with no giving back. Thinking about these events now makes me tremble with shame and remorse. This is one result of residential school. If I could go back in time, I would be doing a lot of apologizing, especially to Barb and the other women I hurt. Maybe they will understand if they read this book.

I did not know what it meant to love someone else, since it was a feeling that was denied to me all those years in residential school. I did love a lot of things in life, but to love another human being was strange. Love was just

95

ARTHUR BEAR CHIEF

not part of my vocabulary. Maybe that's why a lot of good women I met after residential school ran like rabbits once they got a taste of who I was. But it never really bothered me. There were women who wanted to become part of my life, yet I rejected them because I was scared of giving myself for fear I would get hurt in the process. I just did not trust anyone to get close enough to play with my feelings again. I withdrew into my wall of protection and became a scarred child again. I wanted no part of it.

I have come a long way since I first left residential school. During the journey, I have continued to learn new things about myself and why I am the way I am. Awareness, though, does not automatically lead to change. I once asked Marie what she thought of me as an individual when it comes to giving. She said, "You know, Art, you never want to give, but you want to take. On the surface you seem to want to give, but when everything is said and done, you withdraw into your own little world because you are scared of anyone coming too close to you. You are critical of people, but you don't look at yourself first. You hurt people, perhaps not intentionally, and you turn people off. You never really care because all you do is go back into your shell. But what about the people who care about you? They get turned off, so they back away from you, not really knowing your true feelings. You are very cold and uncaring. Sometimes I don't want to be part of you, and other times I don't want to be near you." Those comments hurt me, but they were very true.

Now I can say to myself, "This is what residential school did to me," but then I realize that I still have a long way to go. My inner self is still healing and learning about who I really am. When the day comes that I can talk about my residential school experience without getting misty-eyed or feeling the pain, maybe then I will be getting closer to achieving my journey's goal—to be free of demons. They are like a curse that won't go away. I guess they will stay with me until I die. I try very hard to change my way of thinking, but it seems I always fall back into the way I am. But the day is coming when I will have to face God. I will answer then.

Am I really a bad person? I don't know. I had so much turmoil inside of me that I often wonder how I survived. By all psychological reasons, I should have been dead by now. But when something has been ingrained into you, when it is the only thing you have ever learned since an early age, how can you fight it? A lot of my crying has to do with not knowing how I can come to grips with these feelings and truly overcome them. Before I die, I hope they will be overcome, and I can finally be at peace with myself.

In 2006, when the Assembly of First Nations and the Government of Canada announced the settlement of Indian residential school abuses and how the process was going to work, I said to myself, "All this glorifying of themselves over the biggest class action suit in Canada's history!" I wondered if somewhere in the process, they—the government—would screw up and leave First Nations peoples holding the bag with nothing in it because everybody else had fattened their pockets, and we—the survivors, who suffered the most—would have to fight over the crumbs left behind.

The lawyers certainly did not get poor on us. Quite the contrary! They were the biggest vultures, pretending to speak for us when their only real interest was money. As someone who was abused both physically and sexually, not to mention the mental and emotional scarring I and others have to live with for the rest of our lives, it's an insult to my personal dignity that, throughout this whole settlement process, I and many others had to fight tooth and nail to get any kind of just settlement for our abuses.

The settlement process stirred up a whole lot of pent-up frustration on the part of survivors and, certainly for me, it opened a floodgate when I had to go back to a time in my life I wanted to truly forget. The government thought that by paying us, everything would go away. For me personally, the hurt and the pain that I had long ago locked away in my head came out like flood waters. Having to go through everything again, I can only say that the measly payment I received was an insult to me, but my lawyers told me, "This is the best offer you are likely to get, so we recommend that you accept it. If we go back for more negotiation or go to court, we might get less or lose." With that in mind, I decided to accept the offer. Needless to say, my lawyers took 30 percent for their work.

The whole process was flawed to begin with. Some payouts were higher in some provinces than others. Were their abuses more horrible? I don't think so. So why were the payments different then? Nobody seems to know. After many victims had already filed claims through lawyers, the government decided to introduce the Alternative Dispute Resolution process. In proper planning, it should have been one of the avenues I and others could choose from. Instead we got locked in with law firms and threatened if we released or fired them. We were financially responsible for all work they did on our behalf.

My settlement payment was $105,000. The government only looked at the sexual abuse for payment; they did not touch any other areas, like the physical assaults, the emotional and mental abuses, and the forced confinement. In my opinion, all of them should have been a part of the settlement. By the time I received a cheque, it was only about $69,000. That was supposed to relieve all the pain and erase everything I went through.

I know some survivors from Siksika who were offered settlements and refused them because it was an insult to them to be asked to accept such a pitiful offer. Other individuals who settled through lawyers viewed their payments as a farce but took them anyway. Of course, the lawyers took their 30 percent. My older brother was one of these individuals. I felt sorry for him. When he showed me his statement from the lawyers, I almost cried for him. Others I know of simply refused to accept, and, in one case, the individual sent the cheque back to the government. The response he received basically stated that he had a bad attitude.

The original Alternative Dispute Resolution maximum payout was $245,000, and when that was replaced with the IAP—the so-called Independent Assessment Process—the maximum payout went up to $430,000. The payout differences between the litigations, the ADR, and the IAP were ridiculous. One individual, who spent only three years in residential school, received a settlement of $50,000 through IAP and got to keep all of it. Another received a payment of $150,000 through ADR. For those of us who were in residential school for ten months of the year and not allowed to go home or see our parents for that time period, we received pitiful settlements through our lawyers. I spent ten years at Old Sun, and my actual payout was $69,000. Where is the justice for me and the others like me?

In addition to the litigations, the ADR, and the IAP, the Common Experience Payment was put in place for anyone who attended residential school. The payout was $10,000 for the first year and $3,000 for each year after, but of course it is not that simple. You have to prove you existed for those years, and the government has all the records. In my case, I was told that they had no record that I was at Old Sun Indian Residential School for certain years or whether I was just a day student. If I wanted to prove that I existed, I had to provide names of former staff members and students who were there with me.

I got paid for June 1949 because I was taken to Old Sun, according to policy, on my seventh birthday, which was only a couple of days before the school year ended. I did not, however, get paid for my first full year, 1949–50, because I don't exist in the record. I guess I was already dead but didn't know it! I am sure there are many other survivors who went through similar stonewalling. You expect the payment based on your honest claim, and you are denied a certain amount because of the shabby records and incompetent way of keeping them. Of course, once again, we the survivors have to go through abuse, but now it's financial abuse. The Canadian government should be ashamed of how it has treated the residential school survivors in regards to their claims. In my case, I was basically told that I am a liar because somebody could not locate me in Old Sun records during my first full year. Now I must ask, "How much more punishment can I withstand?" And I am sure this is a question that many others have also asked of themselves.

The Merchant Law Group was the biggest benefactor of the settlement process. It was the most proactive in recruiting clients. A friend told me that he attended a pow-wow where he witnessed lawyers from the firm soliciting for residential school survivors. Is there no honour when it comes to getting on the gravy train at the expense of the people who actually went through the pain and suffering? In my opinion, the Merchant Law Group did a disservice to many survivors by not providing them with the services they deserved. In hindsight, I should have followed through on the advice of my original lawyer, Tom Stepper, the young man who was very insistent that I go to court for my claim. He was confident that I would do very well in court. He was still around for my examination for discovery, and he told me, "We will get a good settlement for you, Art. If not, we will apply to the courts to have it heard." Shortly after that he was banished and eventually released from the firm. When the new lawyer took over from him, one of the first things she told me was, "Your case is not as good as it sounds." Her words upset me, and it seemed from that point on that my relationship with the firm became one of mistrust. I did not have much confidence in her, but I had to suck it up, just like in everything else.

The government's fund for the lawyers across Canada amounted to, if I remember correctly, $25 million. When my settlement came through, I asked the lawyer about the fund and why I was still paying the 30 percent. She said something like, "Oh, that comes in somewhere down the road." I did not question her any further. I just wanted to get my money and get of there as fast as I could, feeling that if I didn't see her ever again, it would be of no consequence to me. If, somewhere down the road, the Merchant Law Group did access the fund for work on my file and got paid for it, I would have to say that the firm was double-dipping and would owe me my 30 percent, which amounts to $32,500 plus the other expenses that were deducted.

As far as I am concerned, the government, churches, and the law firms involved were all part of the system that did nothing but put obstacles in our way to prevent a fair settlement. The biggest hypocrite is the government: it handed out settlement payments for the survivors, but it also charged us GST. My law firm deducted the required

GST from my settlement. How much more can the Government of Canada abuse us?

I am saddened by the whole process where so many people got rich on the residential school survivors, and yet many survivors died before even seeing a penny of their claim. I cry every time I think of those who passed on without ever seeing a payment or justice for themselves. I am bitter about what happened with my settlement, but I can do little to remedy the injustice now. I just consider it to be another chapter in the sad history of how the government treats First Nations peoples.

I and many other survivors were treated without regard of our dignity and self-esteem, making us feel that we are still subhuman and of little value to the country.

I had a lot of resentment in me towards the church and the establishment when I left residential school. I could not comprehend how we could be put through such cruelty and yet no one would stand up to protest our treatment, or even ask what was going on. I believe that the establishment, both the RCMP and Indian Affairs, heard or at least suspected that something was going on. I really don't believe they were stupid or simply did not care. But perhaps they didn't. After all, the government still seems incapable of fair treatment.

Even now, I cannot begin to comprehend a system that was so completely out of whack and so full of individuals who were just there to satisfy their cruelty and lust or understand why they will never be asked to answer for what they did. But that is the justice we survivors have become used to. The federal government policies have failed us. Prime Minister Harper's apology in the House of Commons to the survivors of the residential schools did nothing to overcome our pain and grief for the years of physical, emotional, mental, and sexual abuse we endured at the hands of people who were supposed to look after us while we were taken away from our parents to be sanitized and become white. The recent payouts to supposedly right the wrongs were nothing more than another insult. This is supposed to be "truth and reconciliation"?

The residential school legacy is something the federal government and the churches should hang their heads in shame over because of what they did to thousands of innocent children. But what do we get? "We are sorry. Here is a few thousand dollars for what we did. We are sure the pain will go away in time, and you can move forward." It's the same old story—give money to the Indians, and they will be pacified. Everything will be forgotten in time, and they will move beyond it like everything else, and nobody will ever have to be held accountable for their actions. Our young people should be frightened because it could happen again. I shudder to think that it could, and I cringe in pain when I think of my grandchildren. But history has proven that if you don't learn from past mistakes, the probability of them happening again is there.

Today, you see survivors who are a living testimony. Each of us carries our own scars inside of us, and we deal with them on our own, as we have done in the past. Not many of us seek public reconciliation. Many of us won't even talk openly about what happened to us. Sad to say, we will take it to the grave. No one will ever know the grief and hurt of so many who have passed on.

The effects of residential schools on our Native communities are deeply rooted. We must deal with our unresolved grief as individuals but also collectively, as a community, and begin our journey of healing and recovery. We must do it ourselves. We cannot rely on others who do not understand what we went through. I truly hope that one day all survivors will have an opportunity to sit down and share with fellow survivors their personal experiences, to cry together and hug each other so tightly that no one can ever hurt us again. We would move forward together as one to fight our demons. We would defeat them, and our lives would become whole and normal again.

AFTERWORD

The Burden of Reconciliation

I know how often you have heard words that have been empty of meaning because they have not been accompanied by actions.

MICHAEL PEERS, "Apology to Native People"

In 1996, the Royal Commission on Aboriginal Peoples released its final report, in five volumes. The report envisioned a new relationship between Aboriginal peoples and the Canadian state, one that recognized the rights of Aboriginal peoples to political and cultural autonomy. The report outlined the legislative changes that would be required to formalize this new relationship, such as an Aboriginal Nations Recognition and Government Act and an Aboriginal Parliament Act. It called for a renewal of the treaty process and the rebuilding of Aboriginal nations, including a redistribution of lands and an expansion of the Aboriginal resource base. Underscoring the urgent need for healing and for the restoration of human dignity, it laid out initiatives intended to strengthen Aboriginal communities and to address existing inequities in areas such as housing and living conditions, education, and health care, as well as to establish Aboriginal control over child welfare. It also emphasized the need for capacity building and job creation and for economic development more broadly. In short, the report proposed a reconfiguration of power, in which the Canadian state would be obliged to honour its treaties and abandon its paternalism and colonial control over the lives of those whose lands it occupies.[1]

The commissioners acknowledged that the full implementation of their recommendations would take twenty years. Twenty years have now passed, and most of the commissioners' recommendations have not been implemented. "We must do it ourselves," Arthur declares. He is speaking of community healing, but his words testify to a more pervasive sense of betrayal and abandonment. In recounting his experiences, he does not speak optimistically of reconciliation, nor is it difficult to understand why. His efforts to find a measure of justice have left him angry and embittered, convinced that true compassion—a quality that, ironically, he accuses himself of lacking—is little more in evidence now than it was during his days at Old Sun. Gradually, he is coming to terms with the abuses he suffered at residential school and the impact they had on his personality, his ability to form human relationships, and his professional life. But he is less prepared to forgive those who held out false promises of justice.

Legalism and Restitution

Arthur's search for justice began in 1999, when Tom Stepper, of the Merchant Law Group, arrived in Gleichen, the small Alberta town immediately adjacent to the Siksika reserve. Stepper was there to find clients, and Arthur was one of several who signed up with the firm that evening, on a contingency basis. His decision to take legal action came at the close of a decade during which former students had begun to come forward in ever growing numbers, emboldened by a new public awareness of the reality of residential schools. In October 1990, Phil Fontaine, then the chief of the Assembly of Manitoba Chiefs, revealed on national television that he had been a victim of physical and sexual abuse while a student at Fort Alexander (Pine Falls) Residential School, expressing the hope that his own willingness to speak about his experiences would help others to do the same.[2] At the same time, abusers themselves were beginning to be exposed and convicted of physical and sexual assault, setting off what John Milloy describes as "a chain reaction of police investigations and further prosecutions."[3] Among those subsequently prosecuted was Arthur's own abuser, William Peniston Starr. In 1993, Starr pleaded guilty to ten charges of sexual assault involving young boys at the Gordon Indian Residential School, in Saskatchewan, for which he was sentenced to four and a half years in prison. As later became clear, these ten boys, aged seven to fourteen, represented only a tiny fraction of Starr's victims.[4]

At this time, survivors of abuse had no recourse other than the legal system, and the number of lawsuits steadily escalated, rising especially steeply at the end of the 1990s. By 2000, Arthur was but one of several thousand residential school litigants, and the threat of a successful class action suit loomed on the horizon. As J. R. Miller notes, in responding to individual lawsuits, the Canadian government adopted a policy of cross-suing the church that had been responsible for the residential school named in the case, an action that not only rendered the litigation more complex but "drove several of the churches to the edge of bankruptcy."[5] In addition to the financial implications, the sheer volume of lawsuits clearly posed a problem for the court system. As both the government and the churches recognized, it was critical to find a means to resolution that was equitable but that limited their financial exposure.

In 2001, Prime Minister Jean Chrétien created the federal Office of Indian Residential Schools Resolution Canada, which was charged with managing and resolving claims. This was followed, in November 2003, by the introduction of the National Resolution Framework, which set up an Alternate Dispute Resolution (ADR) process that provided individuals with an alternative to legal action.[6] The ADR option proved to be cumbersome, however, and, inasmuch as his lawsuit was already underway, it was also of no use to Arthur. In fact, after the conclusion of his examination for discovery, in February 2003, Arthur heard nothing of significance from his lawyers, and, as he indicates in his letter to Tom Stepper of 12 May 2003 (see appendix A), he was already becoming more than a little irritated by the lack of progress. Little did he realize then that his wait had only just begun.

In May 2005, the Government of Canada undertook a formal move towards a collective solution to the legacy of residential schools. The government appointed the Honourable Frank Iacobucci, recently retired from the Supreme Court, to enter into negotiations with, on the one hand, legal counsel for the churches that had been responsible for running residential schools and, on the other, legal counsel representing former residential school students, along with a number of Aboriginal organizations, including the Assembly of First Nations and Inuit Tapiriit Kanatami. These negotiations culminated in May 2006, when the Indian Residential Schools Settlement Agreement (IRSSA) was approved by all the parties involved. Legally ratified in March 2007, the agreement went into effect on 19 September 2007. The IRSSA allocated $125 million to the Aboriginal Healing Foundation for measures to support community-based healing, as well as setting aside another $20 million for both national and community commemorative projects. It also established the Truth and Reconciliation Commission, which was provided with a budget of $60 million for the purpose of researching, recording, and preserving the experiences of residential school survivors.[7]

The Truth and Reconciliation Commission was granted no legal authority. Its principal role was not to redress abuse but to document it and, in so doing, to raise public consciousness about residential schools and their legacy, as well as to promote healing. The IRSSA also contained legal provisions for financial restitution, however, of two types. The first was the Common Experience Payment, which any former residential school student could claim, provided that he or she was still alive on 30 May 2005.[8] Claimants were entitled to $10,000 for the first year of residential schooling and $3,000 for each subsequent year—although, as Arthur's experience indicates, the government was not prepared to take the survivor's word for it. Proof of attendance was required, in the form of school records, which were apt to be incomplete and/or inaccurate. Despite the good intentions presumably underlying the CEP, and despite many expressions of sorrow and concern, when it came down to cash, the government was evidently unwilling to include testimony from an Aboriginal person under the rubric of "truth."

The second form of financial compensation—the Independent Assessment Process (IAP)—was intended for victims of physical and/or sexual abuse. The IAP, which was administered by the Indian Residential Schools Adjudication Secretariat, sought to establish a system that would allow compensation to be awarded to thousands of litigants according to a uniform set of criteria, and, by extension, would discourage former residential schools students from pursuing private litigation. Quite apart from the burden placed on the legal system, individual court settlements would create a welter of precedents, which could potentially be used to justify awards of increasing amounts. Under the IAP, the amount of compensation was calculated on the basis of the type of abuse suffered and its severity, as well as the long-term harms that resulted, with the various categories described in detail both in Schedule D of the settlement agreement itself, as well as in the *Guide to the Independent Assessment Process Application*.

Each category was assigned a range of points. For example, in the case of sexual abuse, claimants might be awarded anywhere from 5 to 10 points, for Sexual Abuse Level 1 (SL1), all the way 45 to 60 points, for Sexual Abuse Level 5 (SL5). Depending on its severity, physical abuse (PL) earned a claimant 11 to 25 points. "Harm resulting in some dysfunction" (H4) was good for 16 to 19 points, while 20 to 25 points were awarded for H5, "Continued harm resulting in serious dysfunction" (including psychotic disorganization, loss of ego boundaries, and suicidal tendencies). And so on. Once the assessment was complete, the points were totalled and their dollar value assigned. Claimants earning only 1 to 10 points would receive compensation in the range of $5,000 to $10,000, while claimants who earned more than 121 points would receive a payment in the range of $246,000 to $275,000 (the maximum payment).[9] As the length of the *Guide to the Independent Assessment Process Application*—forty-four pages in its most recent version—might suggest, applying for IAP compensation on one's own was no simple matter.[10] Rather, claimants were advised to retain a lawyer, who would, of course, take a cut of the resulting settlement.

The Indian Residential Schools Settlement Agreement was the outcome not only of the negotiations initiated in May 2005 but also of a class action suit brought in August

2005 by the Assembly of First Nations on behalf of former students—"the biggest class action suit in Canada's history," as Arthur rightly describes it.[11] As in class action suits generally, individuals were given the right to opt out of the settlement, whether because they simply did not wish to receive compensation or because they would prefer to sue privately, in hopes of receiving a better settlement. Otherwise, all former students, even those who had already initiated a private lawsuit, were included in the settlement agreement. The government created a fund for the payment of legal fees, on the understanding that lawyers involved in the settlement would not charge their clients a fee in connection with CEP claims. In the case of claims for abuse, which would now be handled through the IAP, the government agreed to pay lawyers 15 percent of the settlement amount. However, individuals such as Arthur, who had already signed contingency agreements with lawyers, would be obliged to honour those agreements. If the 15 percent payment provided by the government did not cover the total legal fees accrued, the individual would be responsible for paying the balance out of his or her settlement.[12] Individuals were given until 20 August 2007 to opt out of the IRSSA. In the end, relatively few did, but there is no indication that the Merchant Law Group ever informed Arthur of his options.

Almost immediately upon the announcement of a settlement agreement in May 2006, Jane Summers, of the Merchant Law Group, sent a statement of claim on Arthur's behalf to the Edmonton office of the Department of Justice (see appendix A), along with a transcript of Arthur's examination for discovery. On the basis of his earlier testimony, Summers argued that Arthur should be awarded 40 points (roughly in the middle of the SL4 range) for having been sexually assaulted by William Starr and another 18 points (in the SL2 range) for the incident with Starr and Nelson Wolf Leg. She further proposed that Arthur be awarded 19 points for physical abuse (at the top of the PL range) and 15 points (the top of the H3 range) for the resulting harm, for a grand total of 92 points. The compensation proposed was $135,000, for general damages, plus an additional $3,500 for future psychological care.

As a glance at settlement amounts listed in the IRSSA's Schedule D indicates, a total of 92 points falls in the range of 91 to 100 points, for which the recommended compensation is anywhere from $151,000 to $180,000. Arguably, then, the proposed settlement should have been more like $155,000, and it is unclear why Summers chose to ask for only $135,000—a sum that in fact falls below the midpoint of the range for 81 to 90 points ($126,000 to $150,000). Given that Schedule D was finalized in May 2006, it seems unlikely that she was unaware of the compensation amounts it listed. One can only guess, then, that she was hoping for an expeditious settlement, on the assumption that, if the proposed amount had been higher, this might have tempted a government adjudicator to contest the total of 92 points. Arthur is emphatic that the Merchant Group did not consult with him either on the point allocation or on the settlement amount. Had he known that Merchant Law was, in effect, undervaluing his claim, no doubt he would have had something to say on the subject.

firms for their expenses, Merchant Law was still keeping 30 percent of his settlement, he did not receive a clear answer.

The bitterness that Arthur still feels is palpable in his account of his lawsuit. "I and many other survivors were treated without regard of our dignity and self-esteem," he writes, "making us feel that we are still subhuman and of little value to the country." Arthur is bitter in part about the amount of his settlement, which, in the end, was not the $135,000 that Summers originally requested but only $105,000—with Arthur ending up with a mere $69,000.[13] As he points out, it appears that those who pursued settlements entirely through the IAP or through the ADR did considerably better. The fact that the government had the audacity to expect him to pay the GST on the settlement only added insult to injury.

But he is also bitter about the whole approach, which he views as an attempt to buy the Indians off, making him feel "like a whore" for accepting the money at all. Arthur's reaction well illustrates not only the colonization implicit in imposing Western legal principles on people who have their own set of legal traditions, founded on a different way of conceptualizing the world, but also its consequences. Once one accepts the idea that a dollar value can be placed on suffering, the all but inevitable result is competition, in which those who have suffered are encouraged to compare and contrast the size of their suffering, as measured in a sum of money, with the suffering of others.

For roughly a decade, the Merchant Law Group and the Government of Canada have been locked in a legal battle, with the government fighting to recover $25 million paid to the firm in 2008 by court order. It is a war that has no heroes. Having already looked for ways to limit the size of settlements, the government is hoping to avoid having to pay Merchant Law for its services, on the grounds that the firm may (or may not) have been guilty of fraud. For its part, Merchant Law is unable to produce records that would demonstrate that its billing practices were fair and accurate. Inasmuch as allegations on both sides remain unproven, the dispute seems unlikely ever to have a clear resolution.[14] Striking by its absence from this legal saga, however, is evidence of concern for residential school survivors who may have been cheated out of money owed to them. They appear to have been left in the dust, and the spirit of reconciliation is nowhere in sight.

Apology as Insult

The legal system, which assumes the existence of an adversarial relationship between two parties, has little use for apologies. To apologize is to accept responsibility for wrongdoing: it is an admission of guilt. For this reason, defendants are routinely advised to avoid offering any sort of apology. And yet, as we all know, the process of reconciliation often begins with an apology. In *Apologising for Serious Wrongdoing*, a report prepared in 1999 for the Law Commission of Canada, Susan Alter observes, "For a victim, an apology is often considered to be the key that will unlock the door to healing. In light of the importance of apologies to survivors of institutional abuse, it is

unfortunate and disturbing that traditional justice processes foster intransigence, disrespect and lack of remorse
on the part of wrongdoers."[15] In this regard, the IRSSA was
at odds with itself. The processes it put in place to provide
financial restitution operated within the universe of the
legal system, with claimants obliged to present proof of
injury and, in the case of the IAP, to rely on lawyers to make
a case for the gravity of that injury. At the same time, the
settlement agreement set up the Truth and Reconciliation
Commission and included a generous grant to the Aboriginal Healing Foundation.

The Aboriginal Healing Foundation had come into
existence at the end of March 1998, as part of an earlier
government effort to redress the wrongs done to Canada's
Indigenous peoples. In January 1998, Jane Stewart, the
minister of what was then the Department of Indian Affairs and Northern Development, delivered an address
announcing the release of *Gathering Strength—Canada's
Aboriginal Action Plan*, her department's response to the
1996 report of the Royal Commission on Aboriginal
Peoples. Included in her speech was a "Statement of Reconciliation," which also appeared in the printed document.
In it, the Government of Canada acknowledged "the role it
played in the development and administration" of residential schools. The statement also contained the following
apology:

> Particularly to those individuals who experienced
> the tragedy of sexual and physical abuse at residential
> schools, and who have carried this burden believing

that in some way they must be responsible, we wish
to emphasize that what you experienced was not your
fault and should never have happened. *To those of you
who suffered this tragedy at residential schools, we are deeply
sorry.*[16]

Stewart's speech was the first formal apology offered on
behalf of the Canadian government. But it would not be
the last.

In her report to the Law Commission of Canada, Alter
lays out a blueprint for a successful apology, one that sat-
isfies the ultimate goal of making amends, namely, "to
restore dignity and social harmony." Citing psychiatrist
Aaron Lazare, Alter notes that apologies may be prompted
by four possible motives: "(1) to salvage or restore a damaged relationship; (2) to express regret and remorse for
causing someone to suffer and to try to help diminish their
pain; (3) to escape or reduce punishment; and (4) to relieve
a guilty conscience."[17] Multiple motives may be at work
in an apology, of course: the question is one of priorities.
Someone receiving an apology will naturally be alert to
the apparent motive(s), and the perceived sincerity of the
apology will depend on whether the motives seem to the
recipient relatively altruistic or relatively self-serving. In
addition, in the case of an apology delivered on behalf of
an institution, the status of the person chosen to offer it
serves as a signal of its relative importance.

Arthur received two letters of apology, one in November 2006 from the Anglican Church and another, in March
2007, from Indian Residential Schools Resolution Canada

(see appendix B). The first was signed not by the primate—
at the time, the Most Reverend Andrew Hutchison—but
by the general secretary of the church, Archdeacon Michael Pollesel. Similarly, the second came from the office
of the deputy minister, Andrew Harrison, rather than from
the minister himself. Aside from the salutation and the
name of the residential school in question, neither apology contains anything specific to Arthur: both read like
boilerplate letters.

Of the two, the letter from the government is the more
straightforward. It is perhaps most notable for its somewhat
sanctimonious concluding paragraph, which expresses the
hope that, by recounting his painful experiences, Arthur
will achieve "a measure of comfort," enough to enable him
and his family to "move forward" with their lives. Given
that, as a general rule, adult human beings do not wish
for the impossible, simply by giving voice to this hope the
letter implies that the hope is a reasonable one—that its
fulfilment lies within the realm of possibility. In so doing,
it subtly projects blame onto the victim. If, having spoken
out about his pain, Arthur in fact does *not* move forward, he
will have failed in his effort to attain a goal that should be
within his reach. Given that the effects of serious trauma
are not so easily dislodged, this hope for a happy ending
seems disingenuous—if also thoroughly understandable.
After all, if this wish were to come true, it would certainly
do much to relieve the government of its guilt. The letter
also contains three references to "you and your family," a
phrase that contains a whiff of cultural insensitivity, as it

seems to suggest not an extended family but the nuclear, white variety (presumably intact).

The letter from the Anglican Church is considerably more equivocal. Almost imperceptibly, its central paragraph effects a shift in emphasis from the personal to the general—from Arthur as an individual to the abstract mass of children who attended residential schools, among whom Arthur was clearly but one. By pointing out that the church never had "any intention to cause harm or suffering," the letter qualifies its apology, offering something closely akin to an excuse. In addition, it blames the need for an apology on the "few staff" who "took advantage" of the children, in the form of physical or sexual abuse, and then goes on to lament that "your school years, which should have been filled with fun and learning, were instead filled with fear and dread." Implicit in this statement is the suggestion that the standard experience of children at residential schools was one of "fun and learning," with "fear and dread" caused only by a few bad apples. In fact, when one considers that some 38,000 living residential school survivors filed claims under the IAP, one can only conclude that these bad apples kept themselves busy. On the whole, the letter seems concerned less with apologizing than with projecting an image of the church as a worthy and caring institution.

Pollesel's letter makes an especially poor comparison to the apology offered in August 1993 by Archbishop Michael Peers, the primate of the Anglican Church prior to Hutchison. His was a personal apology, delivered at the National Native Convocation directly to those for whom it was most immediately intended. "I have heard with admiration the stories of people and communities who have worked at healing," Peers said, "and I am aware of how much healing is needed. I also know that I am in need of healing, and my own people are in need of healing, and our church is in need of healing. Without that healing, we will continue the same attitudes that have done such damage in the past." His language of his apology was simple:

> I am sorry, more than I can say, that we were part of a system which took you and your children from home and family.
>
> I am sorry, more than I can say, that we tried to remake you in our image, taking from you your language and the signs of your identity.
>
> I am sorry, more than I can say, that in our schools so many were abused physically, sexually, culturally and emotionally.

"We failed you," Peers said. "We failed ourselves. We failed God."[18]

Peers's apology also offers an instructive counterpoint to Stewart's apology, delivered five years later on behalf of the Canadian government. "Sadly, our history with respect to the treatment of Aboriginal people is not something in which we can take pride," Stewart said, perhaps understating the case. Acknowledging that "attitudes of racial and cultural superiority led to a suppression of Aboriginal culture and values," she went on to express "profound regret for past actions of the federal government which have contributed to these difficult pages in the history of our relationship together" and to speak of the need "to find ways to deal with negative impacts that certain historical decisions continue to have in our society today." She also spoke of of the importance of learning from the past. Noting that "reconciliation is an ongoing process," she declared that "in renewing our partnership, we must ensure that the mistakes which marked our past relationship are not repeated."[19]

In contrast to Peers's apology, which was generally perceived as heartfelt, Stewart's statement seemed to lack sincerity. As is often the case in government communications, the language is abstract and guarded. While no doubt the "suppression of Aboriginal culture and values"—or, as some might say, the oppression of Aboriginal peoples—is "not something in which we can take pride," this falls short of saying, for example, that this history is "something of which we are deeply ashamed." Her repeated emphasis on the past seems to imply that the government's assimilationist policies (including, of course, residential schools) were grounded in unenlightened attitudes that have since been abandoned, while it also asserts that these "mistakes" are a matter of history—a feature of "our past relationship." One might also ask what "partnership" once existed that has now to be renewed.

The plan that Stewart unveiled, *Gathering Strength*, received a mixed reception, ranging from cautious optimism to outright skepticism.[20] In contrast to the very specific recommendations laid out in the report of the Royal Commission on Aboriginal Peoples, the plan was rather broad, consisting largely of promises. In her accompanying address, Stewart acknowledged that "our words must be supported by concrete actions," and yet the plan itself, while brimming with statements of good intention, did not itself amount to concrete action. As the months went by following its introduction, optimism began to wane, and not only within the Aboriginal community. In its annual report for 2000, the Canadian Human Rights Commission argued that, while some progress in the area of Aboriginal rights had been made over the past decade, "it has been too little and too slow." Pointing out that *Gathering Strength* was now "several years old," the report deemed it "discouraging that many of the Royal Commission's recommendations have yet to be given the consideration they deserve."[21]

A little over a decade after Stewart offered her "Statement of Reconciliation," the Canadian government made a second attempt at an apology. On 11 June 2008, Canada's then prime minister, Stephen Harper, delivered a speech in the House of Commons in which he formally apologized to Canada's Aboriginal peoples for the harm done to them by the residential school system. "The treatment of children in Indian Residential Schools is a sad chapter in our history," he began, echoing Stewart's remarks. He went on to describe the wrongs that had been committed and to acknowledge that the residential schools policy "has had a lasting and damaging impact on Aboriginal culture, heritage and language." As if in tacit admission that Stewart's earlier effort had failed, he also spoke of the government's recognition that "the absence of an apology has been an impediment to healing and reconciliation." Then, addressing "the approximately 80,000 living former students, and all family members and communities," he offered a new apology:

> The Government of Canada now recognizes that it was wrong to forcibly remove children from their homes and we apologize for having done this. We now recognize that it was wrong to separate children from rich and vibrant cultures and traditions, that it created a void in many lives and communities, and we apologize for having done this. We now recognize that, in separating children from their families, we undermined the ability of many to adequately parent their own children and sowed the seeds for generations to follow, and we apologize for having done this. We now recognize that, far too often, these institutions gave rise to abuse or neglect and were inadequately controlled, and we apologize for failing to protect you.

If solely for its use of repetition, this apology bears an unmistakable resemblance to that of Michael Peers fifteen years earlier.

Admitting that the burden of responsibility is "properly ours as a Government, and as a country," Harper concluded by pointing to the Indian Residential Schools Settlement Agreement, describing it as "new beginning and an opportunity to move forward together in partnership." In his closing words, he declared that the Truth and Reconciliation Commission would contribute to "forging a new relationship between Aboriginal peoples and other Canadians, a relationship based on the knowledge of our shared history, a respect for each other and a desire to move forward together with a renewed understanding that strong families, strong communities and vibrant cultures and traditions will contribute to a stronger Canada for all of us."[22]

Alter argues that, to be successful, an apology must contain five fundamental elements: an acknowledgement of the wrong done; the acceptance of responsibility for that wrong; the expression of "sincere regret and profound remorse"; an assurance that the wrong will not recur; and "reparation through concrete measures."[23] Although someone speaking for a government can express regret and remorse, a government is an abstract entity and, as such, cannot feel anything. How far Stephen Harper (or Jane Stewart) actually experienced a sense of regret and remorse, no one can really know, and, in any case, it is largely beside the point. Harper did not commit the wrongs himself, which were also far removed in time from the apology he offered. When a government apologizes, the sincerity of its regret and the depth of its remorse will ultimately be judged by the final of the five elements: concrete reparations. And, in this respect, the Canadian government has so far done poorly.

The failure of the Harper government to follow through on the implications of its apology to residential school survivors has been widely recognized. "It was as if the prime minister thought that the apology completed the agenda and he could close the residential school file," Miller comments. He continues:

His government took no more measures to implement the commitments in the apology, folded the unit of the civil service that had had responsibility for residential school matters back into the mammoth Indian and Northern Affairs Canada department, and short years later gave notice that it would not extend the life of the Aboriginal Healing Foundation that had been created in 1998 to help survivors and communities cope with the damage residential schooling had caused.[24]

The government also adopted what one legal commentator, writing in June 2013, described as "a strategy of delay" with respect to the Indian Residential Schools Settlement Agreement, "litigating for narrow interpretations of the Agreement, refusing to provide documents to the Truth Commission, and imposing of arbitrary new rules on the process"—a trend she characterized as "moving in the opposite direction from reconciliation."[25]

However moving Harper's apology may have been at the time (and reactions to it varied), his government's subsequent actions successfully rendered it hollow. Once again, promises were made and broken: there was little sign of a "new beginning" or the promised "partnership." Indeed, despite Harper's closing vision, it is debatable how far Aboriginal peoples are prepared to view themselves as "Canadians" whose history is "shared" with that of their oppressors. As Alter observes, an apology that is found to be "insincere, insufficient or otherwise unacceptable can deal a crushing blow to an emotionally scarred survivor."[26] It can, in other words, compound the original injury, deepening resentment and a sense of betrayal, rather than serving as a step towards reconciliation.

The Talking Cure

On 18 December 2015, the Truth and Reconciliation Commission of Canada closed its offices. The commission left in its wake an array of publications, including the six volumes of its final report, all now available on the website of the National Centre for Truth and Reconciliation (NCTR), which was created to continue the work of the commission.[27] In addition to other educational projects, the NCTR has compiled a digital archive that contains statements from some 7,000 survivors, approximately 5 million documents from churches, schools, and the government, an estimated 35,000 photographs, and audio and video recordings of oral testimony and other events sponsored by the TRC—upwards of 200 terabytes of information. The NCTR describes the archive as a "sacred bundle that the NCTR will protect and preserve for all time, for the benefit of all Canadians."[28] According to its mandate, the organization's goal is, in part, to ensure that "survivors and their families have access to their own history."[29]

It is difficult to know what to make of such statements. The assumption seems to be that, without the work of the Truth and Reconciliation Commission and its successor, survivors and their families would not have access to their own history. Undeniably, this "sacred bundle" will be of enormous benefit to researchers and educators. Yet one wonders precisely who, apart from them, will read these millions upon millions of words or how a digital archive will benefit First Nations individuals living on reserves that lack safe drinking water, to say nothing of high-speed Internet connections. In other words, one begins to suspect that this massive record of Indigenous experience has relatively little to do with the realities facing the descendants of those whose testimony it preserves—and, in so preserving, tacitly consigns to the realm of history.

Canada's Truth and Reconciliation Commission was, as Ronald Niezen notes, unusual in a number of respects—in its focus on the abuse of children, for example, and on the psychological impact of institutional trauma. It was also deliberately shorn of legal power, and, unlike many such commissions, was not associated with war crimes or with a change of regime. Instead, the TRC was "an outcome of civil litigation."[30] As Kim Stanton puts it, "the TRC was not created out of a groundswell of concern about IRS survivors by the public," and, as a result, it was obliged to confront "the need to prompt Canadians to invest in and take ownership of a process that they did not instigate."[31] Insofar as the TRC's mission was one of public education, it first had to convince the Canadian public of the value of the proceedings. How far it succeeded in this is a matter of debate. After an initial burst of media attention, public interest predictably waned, and non-Aboriginal attendees at the hearings were apt to be people who already had some knowledge of residential schools and were sympathetic to the situation of survivors.

As part of its mandate, the NCTR similarly seeks to ensure that "the public can access historical records and other materials to help foster reconciliation and healing." But, quite apart from restrictions on access required in the interests of privacy, one also wonders how many members of the public will take the time not merely to access these materials but to reflect on them. That is, one wonders about the mechanism whereby such archiving will contribute to reconciliation, if by "reconciliation" we mean the process of achieving some measure of emotional rapport and mutual understanding between settler Canadians and those they so grievously injured. Rather, this massive exercise in the documentation of abuse seems to share something of the character of rituals of expiation. If we (the colonizers) can amass a sufficiently thorough catalogue of our sins, thereby offering a full confession, surely then our guilt will be absolved. We will then be reconciled to ourselves, at which point we can breathe freely again, put the past behind us, and assume no further responsibility for present-day realities.[32]

Implicit in the TRC process was the assumption that telling one's story is the first step towards healing—what Niezen describes as the commission's "goal of healing through self-revelation."[33] The notion that, left unspoken, secrets fester and make us ill has acquired the status of common wisdom (at least in Western cultures), as has its corollary, namely, that personal unburdening is cleansing and cathartic. And yet, as Niezen points out, the ubiquitous presence of health support workers at the TRC hearings testified to the commission's recognition that telling one's story (or hearing the stories of others) can serve as a "trigger," bringing about an emotionally devastating re-awakening of the original trauma. Special concern focused on Private Statement Gathering, sessions during which a survivor could delve into his or her memories in as much detail as desired—a process the commission identified as "a locus of particularly intense emotion with an accompanying high risk of sudden-onset mental health crises." As a result, health support workers were "on hand to sit with statement providers throughout their interviews," and the interviewee could also invite "personal supports" to be present.[34]

Arthur Bear Chief chose not to take part in the TRC hearings. He had already told his story, in circumstances so humiliating as to transform the process of self-revelation into a further act of abuse. Counsellors who work with victims of trauma are well aware of the possibility of re-traumatization, and one could very reasonably argue that lawyers should have at least a passing acquaintance with the concept—or, if nothing else, have enough common sense to recognize that recounting experiences of serious physical and emotional abuse could be quite upsetting. One could, in fact, argue that it was morally irresponsible to demand that Arthur relive his experiences without prior advice from a counsellor, who should also have been present in the room. As Arthur's account of his reaction illustrates, the risk of suicide is very real. Not that voluntarily testifying at TRC hearings was anything equivalent to Arthur's examination for discovery, of course, but one can readily understand why he might be reluctant to participate in the proceedings.

Another factor may, however, have been at work in the decision of some survivors to forgo participation in TRC events. In the vast documentary record generated by the TRC, the individual voice is easily overwhelmed. Although comfort can be found in the realization that one was not alone in one's suffering, the generalization of pain tends to deflect attention from the lived reality of individual trauma. Indeed, the focus of the commission arguably fell on collective trauma and, by extension, on collective, rather than personal, healing. As Niezen observes, it is unclear whether "giving testimony can maintain the effects of a sense of common belonging in the absence of consistent, effective therapeutic support."[35] In this respect, the purpose of self-revelation must be interpreted not in the context of individual healing, of the sort associated with the confession of sins, but as a means of giving voice to the experience of historical trauma, which is, in its very nature, the outcome of shared suffering. In other words, self-revelation must be understood as part of a process in which those victimized by the wrongs of others are finally given an opportunity to speak out—to arrive at a collective truth and thus to create a counternarrative, from which they can hopefully draw strength.

To those who stand outside a community of sufferers, those who have no experiential basis of understanding, the notion of historical trauma tends to remain an abstract concept, lacking tangibility. Perhaps for that reason alone, its impact is far more easily ignored or dismissed than that of an individual voice, one that speaks of personal pain. While Arthur's narrative well illustrates the manner in which trauma is transmitted across generations, its power attaches more to its capacity to concretize historical trauma, to give it shape and substance. His memories are also offered in the spirit of Indigenous storytelling, which is always a two-way process that places a burden of responsibility on the listener.

In any oral tradition, storytelling is, above all, a mode of teaching. As such, storytelling—or what Jo-ann Archibald aptly terms "storywork"—is oriented more towards the future than the present: stories are told for future generations. Even when the story told is drawn from personal experience, its recounting is intended not to address the current emotional needs of the teller but to impart knowledge, knowledge that may someday evolve into wisdom. It is expected that those who listen to a story will do so respectfully and thoughtfully, giving the speaker's words their undivided attention. It is also the responsibility of listeners to reflect on the story, seeking to understand and deepen its message in relation not only to their own lives but to the network of relationships within which human beings exist. In *Blackfoot Ways of Knowing*, Betty Bastien explains that knowledge consists in "communicating with the natural and cosmic world of *Siksikaitsitapi* and integrating the knowledge that transpires into one's own being." As she observes, "knowing results from being aware, observant, and reflective."[36]

Such an understanding of story stands in obvious contrast to contemporary notions of "telling one's story" as a means of personal catharsis, in which the focus falls on the teller, while the listener (assuming one is present at all) is expected to do little other than offer expressions of sympathy.[37] In traditional oral storytelling, teller and listener exist instead in a reciprocal relationship, and both are reshaped, however subtly, by the exchange. By retelling the story within the context of his or her own experiences, the listener imbues it with new life, with the results that the meaning of the story is endlessly reinterpreted and reconfigured. It is no surprise that, in addition to writing down his memories, Arthur recounted them orally as well, in the presence of a listener, often elaborating on what he had initially written. He understood, whether consciously or not, that storytelling is an open-ended dialogue, a process that may have a beginning but ideally will not have an end.

It may seem that, by choosing to publish his story as a book, Arthur has frozen it in time. Although his journey of healing is far from over, readers cannot know its future. But then no story is ever complete. Arthur's lived story will evolve, and so will his written story, which will have its own future. It will reach a far wider audience, and it will affect others in ways that cannot be predetermined. Like listeners, readers have a responsibility not only to approach Arthur's story with respect and open themselves up to his words but to ponder the relationship between his story and their own lives—to find in his experiences truths about themselves. Readers are also responsible for "retelling" the story by sharing what they learn with others. In this way, what is written will become oral. It will not be tucked away in an archive. As any story should, it will live and grow—and in that there is hope of reconciliation.

Frits Pannekoek

Notes

1 For a detailed overview of the report, see "Highlights from the Report of the Royal Commission on Aboriginal Peoples," Indigenous and Northern Affairs Canada, https://www.aadnc-aandc.gc.ca/eng/1100100014597/1100100014637 (last modified 15 September 2010). See also Mary C. Hurley and Jill Wherrett, "The Report of the Royal Commission on Aboriginal Peoples," *In Brief*, 4 October 1999 (revised 2 August 2000), Parliamentary Research Branch, Library of Parliament, http://www.lop.parl.gc.ca/content/lop/researchpublications/prb9924-e.htm.

2 Fontaine spoke about his experiences in an interview with Barbara Frum on the CBC program *The Journal*, which is available in the CBC Digital Archives, http://www.cbc.ca/archives/entry/phil-fontaines-shocking-testimony-of-sexual-abuse. The Fort Alexander school, located in southeastern Manitoba on what is today the reserve of the Sagkeeng First Nation, was run by the Missionary Oblates of Mary Immaculate. Just prior to his interview with Frum, Fontaine had spoken with representatives of the Catholic Church about the need to investigate abuses at the school.

3 John S. Milloy, *A National Crime: The Canadian Government and the Residential School System, 1879 to 1986* (Winnipeg: University of Manitoba Press, 1999), 297–98. As Milloy notes, the first wave of convictions, in 1989 and 1990, coincided with revelations surrounding the physical and sexual abuse of non-Aboriginal children at an orphanage in St. John's, Newfoundland, the Mount Cashel Boy's Home, and at the St. Joseph's Training School, in Alfred, Ontario, both operated by a Catholic lay order known as the Christian Brothers. Aboriginal accounts of abuse at residential schools thus dovetailed with mounting concern,

among non-Aboriginal Canadians, about the victimization
of children in institutional settings (298).

4 Starr served as the director of the residential school on the
Gordon reserve (located to the north of Regina) from 1968
to 1984. On the Gordon scandal, see Murray Mandryk,
"Uneasy Neighbours: White-Aboriginal Relations and
Agricultural Decline," in *Writing Off the Rural West:
Globalization, Governments and the Transformation of Rural
Communities*, edited by Roger Epp and Dave Whitson
(Edmonton: University of Alberta Press and the Parkland
Institute, 2001), 210–11.

5 J. R. Miller, "Residential Schools and Reconciliation,"
ActiveHistory.ca, 19 February 2013, http://activehistory.
ca/papers/history-papers-13/, para. 9. For contemporary
reportage, see, for example, James Brooke, "Indian Lawsuits
on School Abuse May Bankrupt Canada Churches,"
New York Times, 2 November 2000, http://www.nytimes.
com/2000/11/02/world/indian-lawsuits-on-school-abuse-
may-bankrupt-canada-churches.html?_r=0.

6 On the ADR process, see Jennifer J. Llewellyn, "Dealing
with the Legacy of Native Residential School Abuse
in Canada: Litigation, ADR and Restorative Justice,"
University of Toronto Law Journal 52, no. 3 (Summer 2002):
253–300. The ADR process offered two models, with
claimants obliged to choose one or the other. Model A
covered claims for serious physical abuse (defined as abuse
resulting in injuries that lasted more than six weeks and/
or required hospitalization or sustained medical treatment)
and sexual abuse; Model B was intended for claims involving
less serious physical abuse and/or wrongful confinement.
Awards under Model A ranged from $5,000 to $245,000;
the maximum award under Model B was $3,500. "Apply
for Alternative Dispute Resolution," n.d., http://www.

survivingthepast.ca/robohelp/aboriginalResidentialAbuse
/!SSL!/WebHelp/3-4.1_Apply_for_Alternative_Dispute_
Resolution.htm.

7 For an overview of the settlement, see "Indian
   Residential Schools," Indigenous and Northern
   Affairs Canada, https://www.aadnc-aandc.gc.ca/
   eng/1100100015576/1100100015577 (last modified 24
   August 2016).

8 The IRSSA set aside $1.9 billion for the CEP, with an
   application deadline of 19 September 2011. "Common
   Experience Payments," Indigenous and Northern
   Affairs Canada, http://www.aadnc-aandc.gc.ca/
   eng/1100100015594/1100100015595 (last modified 22
   April 2013). As of 31 March 2016, payments totalling
   upwards of $1.6 billion ($1,622,422,106) had been made.
   "Common Experience Payment (CEP) Map," Indigenous
   and Northern Affairs Canada, http://www.aadnc-aandc.
   gc.ca/eng/1353514851338/1353514981910 (last modified 5
   June 2016).

9 For a full description, see *Schedule "D": Independent Assessment
   Process (IAP) for Continuing Indian Residential Schools Abuse
   Claims*, May 2006, http://www.residentialschoolsettlement.
   ca/schedule_d-iap.pdf, 3–6. The deadline for applications
   was 19 September 2012. A total of 38,094 claims were
   received, of which 35,730 (94%) had been resolved as of 31
   August 2016. At that point, payments totalled $3.048 billion.
   "Adjudication Secretariat Statistics," Indian Residential
   Schools Adjudication Secretariat, 31 August 2016, http://
   www.iap-pei.ca/information/stats-eng.php.

10 See *Guide to the Independent Assessment Process Application*,
   v3.2, 4 April 2013, http://www.iap-pei.ca/information/
   publication/pdf/pub/iapg-v3.2-20130404-eng.pdf, esp.
   34–37.

11 On the AFN's action, see Paul Barnsley, "AFN Launches Class Action Lawsuit," *Windspeaker*, September 2005, 8, http://www.ammsa.com/publications/windspeaker/ afn-launches-class-action-lawsuit.

12 See the "The Indian Residential Schools Settlement Has Been Approved," http://www.residentialschoolsettlement.ca/ detailed_notice.pdf, 4 (question 9) and 8 (questions 32–34). This is the "Detailed Notice" available on the website of the Indian Residential Schools Adjudication Secretariat, http://www.residentialschoolsettlement.ca/english_index. html, where one can also find a copy of the full settlement agreement.

13 As it happens, $105,000 is the uppermost amount in the 61-to-70-point range, which suggests that, in the final analysis, Arthur "earned" only 70 points. Moreover, given the amount that he ultimately received ($69,000), the Merchant Law Group must have retained roughly 34 percent of the total settlement—possibly 30 percent plus tax.

14 The debate began even before the IRSSA was signed, when Tony Merchant claimed to Frank Iacobucci that the federal government would owe his firm $80 million for services to more than seven thousand residential school clients between 1997 and 2005. Iacobucci had his doubts about the accuracy of the firm's records, and, on 20 November 2005, he and Merchant signed an agreement laying out the verification process to which the firm's legal fees would be subject. The agreement—which was appended to the IRSSA as Schedule V ("Agreement Between the Government of Canada and the Merchant Law Group Respecting the Verification of Legal Fees," available at http://www.residentialschoolsettlement. ca/ScheduleV.pdf)—stipulated that if the two parties were unable to agree on an appropriate amount, the matter

would be settled by binding arbitration but that the final amount "shall in no event be more than $40 million or less than $25 million." After disputes arose, a Saskatchewan court decision in August 2008 ordered the government to pay the firm $25 million, even in the absence of adequate verification. The government proved unwilling to let the matter rest, however, and a subsequent court decision ordered Merchant Law to provide the government with billing statements in support of its claims. This the firm was ultimately unable to do in a manner satisfactory to the government. Early in 2015, the government filed a civil suit demanding that the firm repay the $25 million, whereupon Merchant Law filed a countersuit, arguing that instead the firm was owed an additional $20 million. As this book goes to press, the case is before the Saskatchewan Court of Appeal, which has reserved its decision—although it seems highly unlikely that, whatever the final outcome, Arthur (and others) will ever receive reimbursement for fees paid out of pocket. On the history of the dispute, see Jonathon Gatehouse, "The Residential Schools Settlement's Biggest Winner: A Profile of Tony Merchant," *Maclean's*, 11 September 2006, reprinted 4 April 2013, http://www. macleans.ca/news/canada/white-mans-windfall-a-profile-of-tony-merchant/. See also Bonnie Allen, "Tony Merchant's Law Firm Files Lawsuit Against Ottawa Following $25M Claim," *CBC News*, 30 January 2015 (updated 2 February 2015), http://www.cbc.ca/news/canada/saskatchewan/ tony-merchant-s-law-firm-files-lawsuit-against-ottawa-following-25m-claim-1.2937297; Sarah Kraus, "Merchant Law Group in Legal Battle of Its Own," *Global News*, 30 January 2015 (updated 5 October 2016), http://globalnews. ca/news/1804029/merchant-law-group-in-legal-battle-of-its-own/; and Barb Pacholik, "Ottawa Wants Back Millions Paid to Merchant Law Firm for Residential School Work,"

Regina Leader-Post, 4 October 2016, http://leaderpost.com/
news/local-news/ottawa-trying-again-to-claw-back-25-
million-from-merchant-law-firm-from-residential-school-
work.

15 Susan Alter, *Apologising for Serious Wrongdoing: Social,
Psychological and Legal Considerations*, Final Report for the
Law Commission of Canada, May 1999, https://dalspace.
library.dal.ca/handle/10222/10273, 2.

16 *Gathering Strength—Canada's Aboriginal Action Plan*
(Ottawa: Minister of Public Works and Government
Services Canada, 1997), http://www.ahf.ca/downloads/
gathering-strength.pdf, 3; emphasis in the original. The
full text of Stewart's address, delivered on 7 January 1998, is
available on the website of Indigenous and Northern Affairs
Canada, at https://www.aadnc-aandc.gc.ca/eng/1100100015
725/1100100015726.

17 Alter, *Apologising for Serious Wrongdoing*, 3. Alter cites
Aaron Lazare, "Go Ahead, Say You're Sorry," *Psychology
Today*, January–February 1995.

18 "Apology to Native People: A Message from the Primate,
Archbishop Michael Peers, to the National Native
Convocation, Minaki, Ontario, Friday, August 6, 1993."
The text of Peers's apology is available in twelve languages
on the website of the Anglican Church of Canada, at http://
www.anglican.ca/tr/apology/.

19 *Gathering Strength—Canada's Aboriginal Action Plan*, 2, 3.

20 See, for example, Paul Barnsley, "'Gathering Strength'
Not Strong Enough," *Windspeaker*, February 1998, 2,
http://www.ammsa.com/publications/saskatchewan-sage/
gathering-strength-not-strong-enough.

21 Canadian Human Rights Commission, *Annual Report,
2000* (Ottawa: Minister of Public Works and Government

Services, 2001), 7. See also the "Commentary" section
in Hurley and Wherrett, "The Report of the Royal
Commission on Aboriginal Peoples," which notes concerns
expressed in December 1998 by the United Nations
Committee on Economic, Social and Cultural Rights and,
in February 1999, by the United Nations Human Rights
Committee.

22 The text of Harper's speech is available on the website
of Indigenous and Northern Affairs Canada, https://
www.aadnc-aandc.gc.ca/eng/1100100015644/11001000
15649. For a close reading, see Matthew Dorrell, "From
Reconciliation to Reconciling: Reading What 'We Now
Recognize' in the Government of Canada's 2008 Residential
Schools Apology," *English Studies in Canada* 35, no. 1
(March 2009): 27–45.

23 Alter, *Apologising for Serious Wrongdoing*, 14.

24 Miller, "Residential Schools and Reconciliation," para. 11.

25 Kathleen Mahoney, "The Indian Residential School
Settlement: Is Reconciliation Possible?" *ABlawg.ca*
(University of Calgary, Faculty of Law), 26 June 2013,
http://ablawg.ca/wp-content/uploads/2013/06/Blog_KM_
Settlement_June2013.pdf, 4.

26 Alter, *Apologising for Serious Wrongdoing*, 2.

27 Released in 2015, the six-volume final report of the TRC—
*Canada's Residential Schools: Final Report of the Truth and
Reconciliation Commission of Canada* (available at http://www.
trc.ca/websites/trcinstitution/index.php?p=890 and in print
from McGill-Queen's University Press)—is the definitive
history of Canada's Indian residential schools policy. Also well
worth reading is an earlier report, *They Came for the Children*
(2012). All the TRC's publications can be accessed through
the NCTR's website, at http://nctr.ca/reports.php. The

creation of a research centre that would preserve a permanent record of the commission's work was part of the mandate of the Truth and Reconciliation Commission, as laid out in Schedule N of the Indian Residential Schools Settlement Agreement, http://www.residentialschoolsettlement.ca/ schedule_n.pdf: see article 3 (d) and article 12.

28 "Our Future—Canada's Indigenous Archive," National Centre for Truth and Reconciliation, 2016, http:// umanitoba.ca/centres/nctr/future.html; see also the NCTR's "About" page, at http://nctr.ca/about.php. Regarding the contents of the archive, see "Terabytes of Testimony: Digital Database of Residential School Stories Opens to the Public," *Unreserved, with Rosanna Deerchild*, CBC Radio, 1 November 2015, http://www.cbc.ca/radio/ unreserved/opportunities-for-reconciliation-pop-up-in-unexpected-places-1.3294030/terabytes-of-testimony-digital-database-of-residential-school-stories-opens-to-the-public-1.3296657.

29 "Our Mandate," National Centre for Truth and Reconciliation, 2016, http://umanitoba.ca/centres/nctr/ mandate.html. In addition to public testimony from survivors, the NCTR has been seeking to preserve transcripts of private testimony provided by approximately 38,000 survivors who filed claims for compensation under the Independent Assessment Process (IAP). In August 2014, the Ontario Superior Court of Justice ruled that these documents should be destroyed unless a claimant specifically requested that his or her records be preserved, and in April 2016 the Ontario Court of Appeals upheld this decision, which the TRC had challenged. See "Ontario Court of Appeal Upholds Decision on Destruction of IAP Documents" Indian Residential Schools Adjudication Secretariat, 2016, http://www.iap-pei.ca/media-room/ media-eng.php?act=2016-04-04-eng.php. For background,

see "IAP Records Disposition," Indian Residential Schools Adjudication Secretariat, n.d., http://www.iap-pei.ca/records/main-eng.php; and "The IAP Records," National Centre for Truth and Reconciliation, 2016, http://umanitoba.ca/centres/nctr/iap_records.html.

30 See Ronald Niezen, *Truth and Indignation: Canada's Truth and Reconciliation Commission on Indian Residential Schools* (Toronto: University of Toronto Press, 2013), 3–6; the quotation is from p. 3. The mandate of the TRC specified that the commission "shall not hold formal hearings, nor act as a public inquiry, nor conduct a formal legal process" and "shall not possess subpoena powers" (Indian Residential Schools Settlement Agreement, *Schedule "N": Mandate for the Truth and Reconciliation Commission*, article 2 [b] and [c]).

31 Kim Stanton, "Canada's Truth and Reconciliation Commission: Settling the Past?" *International Indigenous Policy Journal* 2, no. 3 (August 2011): 4.

32 In *Unsettling the Settler Within: Indian Residential Schools, Truth Telling, and Reconciliation in Canada* (Vancouver: University of British Columbia Press, 2011), Paulette Regan argues that settler Canadians cannot meaningfully take part in reconciliation without assuming responsibility for cleansing themselves of their own comforting colonial assumptions. Although the home page of the now-archived TRC website ("Thank You for Visiting trc.ca," Truth and Reconciliation Commission of Canada, n.d. [2015], http://www.trc.ca/websites/trcinstitution/index.php?p=905) announces that "the journey of Truth and Reconciliation is far from over," the NCTR faces a challenge similar to that with which the TRC was originally confronted: it must persuade settler Canadians to continue on that journey.

33 Niezen, *Truth and Indignation*, 110.

34 Ibid., 106. Concerns about possible retraumatization were, and still are, evident in warnings and telephone numbers of 24-hour crisis hotlines printed on relevant documents, such as the *Guide to the Independent Assessment Process Application*, and also posted on web pages. See, for example, the "Indian Residential Schools" page on the website of Indigenous and Northern Affairs Canada, https://www.aadnc-aandc.gc.ca/eng/1100100015576/1100100015577.

35 Niezen, *Truth and Indignation*, 111.

36 Betty Bastien, *Blackfoot Ways of Knowing: The Worldview of the Siksikaitsitapi* (Calgary: University of Calgary Press, 2004), 5. The term *Siksikaitsitapi* means "Blackfoot-speaking real people," that is, those Niitsitapi ("real people") whose native tongue is Siksikaitsipowahsin, the Blackfoot language.

37 This conception of storytelling, as intended to produce catharsis in the teller, is at odds with the ancient Greek model of catharsis, elaborated most extensively in the context of drama. In this model, which is arguably far closer to the Indigenous model, the telling of a story aims to produce catharsis not in the teller but in the audience, whose members respond emotionally to the events portrayed or described.

Legal Correspondence

Eau Claire Place II
#340, 521 3rd Avenue SW
Calgary, Alberta, Canada T2P 3T3

CHRISTOPHER T. THAN

February 18, 2003   Our File No.: 395304

Field Atkinson Perraton LLP
Barristers & Solicitors
#2000, 10235 – 101st St.
Edmonton, AB T5J 3G1

Dear Sir/Madam:

Re: Merchant Law Group Candidate for Test Trial Plaintiffs

1.   Name: Arthur Bear Chief;
2.   Action No.: 9901-03253;
3.   Defendants: Attorney General of Canada and William
     Starr;
4.   Third Parties: The General Synod of the Anglican
     Church of Canada, The Missionary Society of the
     Anglican Church of Canada, The Synod of the Diocese of
     Calgary and William Starr;
5.   Age: June 25, 1942 (60 years old);
6.   Gender: Male;
7.   School: Old Sun's Residential School, Gleichen, Alberta;
8.   Period of Placement: 1949–1959 (10 years);
9.   Status: Status Indian;
10. Treaty Area: Treaty 7;
11. Language: Blackfoot;

12.   Cultural Abuse prior to Residential Schools taught: Sun Dance: Tobacco dance; The Holy Hand Game; Three Grass drumming; Grandmother's second husband, Little Light, Medicine Bundle Holder, was allowed to observe; Ghost Dance (witness); Plaintiff did not speak English prior to Residential School attendance;

13.   Sexual Abuse: William Starr;

14.   Physical Abuse: Unknown female and male supervisors – Reverend Cole, William Starr, Robert Jones (Supervisor, Assistant to William Starr), Captain Tremaine (Teacher);

15.   Reasons for Selection: This Plaintiff is a victim of William Starr - Physical/Sexual abuse. The opportunity to connect liability with the Federal Government and the Anglican Church, which were convicted perpetrators, is great. This gentleman is an excellent witness who is incredibly well-spoken and is very intelligent. Mr. Bear Chief is beginning to understand what has happened to him and how it has affected his life. We anticipate. that by the time of trial, this Plaintiff will be able to intelligently present to the Court his Residential School experiences and how they have affected him throughout his life to the fullest extent possible.

Yours truly,

MERCHANT LAW GROUP

CHRISTOPHER T. THAN
CTT/sdg

May 12, 2003

MERCHANT LAW GROUP
Barristers and Solicitors
#200, 521 – 3rd avenue S.W.
Calgary, Alberta. T2P 3T3

Attention Mr. Tom Stepper

I was told that you are going to be away until the end of May.
I did speak with your new assistant, who did not have any
knowledge of my case, so she could not help me.

Tom, I will not sit on my thumb all summer waiting for the
government to come up with a reasonable settlement offer.
Either they seriously negotiate, with you pushing, or I am
prepared to go to court and I will not wave my rights to any
portions of my claim if it goes that far.

I am tired of waiting. I have gone through a lot and to add
to the insult I have to beg practically on my hands and knees
to get anything from the government and the church. That to
me insults me as a human being of worth who did not ask for
all of this to happen.

I will wait and if there is no significant movement on the
government part then I will definitely give you a time frame
to work with.

Tom, you have to actively push this to determine if they
want to settle it with good faith.

When you get back from your holidays please call me. I
look forward to hearing from you.

Yours Truly
Arthur Bear Chief

MERCHANT LAW GROUP
Eau Claire Place II, #340, 521 3 Avenue, SW
Calgary, Alberta, Canada T2P 3T3

June 1, 2006

"WITHOUT PREJUDICE"

Department of Justice
Edmonton Office
211, 10199 - 101 Street
Edmonton, Alberta T5J 3Y4

Attn: Graham Laschuk, Counsel

Dear Sir:

RE: BEARCHIEF, Arthur *v* Attorney General of Canada et al
   Old Sun Residential School — 9901 03253

Arthur Bearchief attended the Old Sun Residential School
from 1949 to 1959. He also attended St. Paul's Residential
School for 4 months from September to December 1959.

We are enclosing the following:
  1.   Psychologist Report — Donna Gould.
  2.   Treatment notes of Gleichen Medical Centre dated
       January 15, 2003 and treatment notes of Gleichen
       Medical Centre dated May 12, 2006.

**PHYSICAL ABUSE — WILLIAM STARR/ROBERT JONES/
CAPTAIN TREMAINE**

1.   William Starr
     Sunday was known as "Pay Day" as any students who
     had acquired demerit marks (i.e. for speaking Blackfoot)

were made to strip Sunday night in the dorm and were strapped on the buttocks by William Starr. Arthur would have red welts after the strappings. One time Arthur received 15 lashes and had trouble sitting for a week. Mr. Bearchief does not recall any Sunday when he was not strapped. William Starr was at Old Sun for 4–5 years (1950–1955) so that was how long the Sunday strappings continued. ((Transcript) T00123)

In addition he was strapped on the hands by William Starr on average of 2–3 times per week. (T00117–00120)

2. He was also terrorized by Robert Jones.
   On one occasion Arthur and about 20 boys were threatened by Robert Jones while in the playroom. (Robert Jones was an assistant to William Starr). During the incident in the playroom Robert Jones had a gun and was accompanied by a large black dog and asked the boys if "anyone was man enough to come through him." (T00120-00122)

   On another occasion Arthur saw William Starr hold Ralph Stimson in a head-lock during which time he punched Ralph in the face. The older boys were held at bay during the attack by Robert Jones with his gun.

3. Captain Tremaine
   Arthur witnessed Captain Tremaine pounding George Turning Calf's face into the wall 5–6 times until the wall was covered with blood. (T00125)

   Arthur Bearchief was slapped around the head by Captain Treamine a couple of times. (T00127)

Mr. Bearchief indicated that he has suppressed many incidents over the years but that he remembered that the beatings were a regular occurrence. (T00127)

SEXUAL ASSAULT (T00128–T00130)

Arthur was sexually assaulted by William Starr on two occasions.

1. William Starr came into the dormitory where Arthur slept in a bed with his friend Nelson Wolf Leg, William Starr got into bed with both of them. Arthur remembers William Starr forcing him to fondle his penis and once he had a full erection he made Arthur sit on top of him with Starr's penis between Arthur's legs while he moved up and down during which time he continued to fondle Nelson Wolf Leg. After Starr ejaculated the boys were made to rub the ejaculated liquid over Starr's body and over themselves. The next morning they both were given bags of candy.

Nelson and Arthur made a pact to never talk about anything that happened until one or the other was dead. Nelson died an alcoholic on the streets of Calgary and had spent much of his life in jail.

2. After the first incident, William Starr came and took Nelson from the bed and took him into his room, despite the fact that Arthur tried to hold onto Nelson. (T00133–00134)

    The boys in the dorm room always knew who had been taken at night by Starr as whoever the boy happened to be he always had a bag of candy the next morning. (T00135)

3. Arthur was taken from his bed by William Starr when he was 9 or 10 years of age and taken to Starr's room. He remembers Starr fondling him and partially penetrating him from behind but Arthur cried so much that Starr made Arthur cross his legs and Starr ejaculated all over him. **(T00139)** When Starr fell asleep Arthur returned to his bed and he and Nelson cried. **(T00136)**

Arthur received a bag of candy after the incident. **(T00138)**

The first person Arthur spoke to about the abuse was Tom Stepper of the Merchant Law Group. Arthur saw a psychologist, Donna Gould, and spent a lot of his time during his sessions with Ms. Gould crying as he relived the incidents of sexual abuse. **(T00140 & 141)**

SEXUAL ASSAULT and HARM

We further submit that the two incidents of sexual abuse by William Starr are credible as they indicate a similar "modus operandi" of Starr, a convicted pedophile with hundreds of assaults.

Donna Gould, Psychologist, says that it seems likely that he suffered with symptoms of post-traumatic stress disorder as a child, adolescent, and adult.

"Arthur reports continuing to have had nightmares and flashbacks of the sexual abuse as an adult. He subsequently turned to alcohol to cope with the traumatic memories. The results of the Index of Self-Esteem reveal that Arthur's self-esteem is so damaged that he is at risk for depression. He has become aware of the legacy of the unresolved abuse issues, especially as it related to his barriers to intimacy and use of alcohol to cope with the symptoms of Post-traumatic Stress Disorder. Arthur still feels 'dirty' after participating in consensual adult sexual activity. He has overcome many difficulties even though the abuses he endured left him unable to trust most others. Left in the wake are two broken marriages, estranged children, low self-esteem, and alcohol dependency."

PHYSICAL ASSAULT

When Arthur was married to his second wife, Barb, he began to realize the impact Residential School had on him. He had nightmares and woke up screaming "don't hurt me." **(T00167)**

Arthur had problems with alcohol requiring attendance at a Treatment Centre (see Doctor's notes). **(T00168)**

After completing two years of Social Work (1970–1973) Arthur stated, "I started realizing, I started making connections and I said to myself maybe because of what I went through, maybe that's what's affecting me. Maybe I need to deal with the past. But I never did that then."

PROPOSAL

PHYSICAL ASSAULT

We submit that the weekly strappings Arthur received were beyond the standard of the day. Being terrorized and threatened at gunpoint by Robert Jones and his dog was also outside the standard of the day. Witnessing Ralph Stimson being pummeled by Starr, (resulting in Starr's termination) and witnessing a fellow student's head being pounded into the wall by Captain Tremaine would be traumatizing events for a young Arthur.

Level of Abuse	Acts proven	Compensation Points
Sexual abuse Level 4	Taken to Starr's room, partially penetrated.	40
Sexual abuse Level 2	Incident with Starr and Nelson Wolf Leg in the bed. Simulated intercourse, fondling under clothing.	18
Physical abuse Level 3	Hit on bare buttocks weekly for 4–5 years. Strapped 2–3 times per week by Starr. Slapped on the side of the head. Terrorized and threatened with a gun	19
Harm (Please see psychologists' report)	Nightmares. Alcohol abuse. Difficulty relating to others. Low self-esteem. Searching for help through alcohol treatment centre, self-study and Psychological counselling.	15

TOTAL POINTS   92

FUTURE CARE

Donna Gould, Psychologist recommends a further 15–20 hours of counselling.
Psychologists are now charging from $175.00 per hour in Alberta, therefore we require further funds for counselling in the amount of $3,500.00.

We would recommend settlement of:

General damages	$135,000.00
Future care	$3,500.00
Plus Interest	
Plus costs & Disbursements	

We would remind you that our client now has Picks Disease (a form of dementia). The Statement of Claim was filed in 1999 and Examination for Discovery took place in October 2002. Our client is anxious to resolve this matter and seek further counselling.

Thank you for your immediate attention to this proposal.

Yours truly,
MERCHANT LAW GROUP

JANE ANN SUMMERS
JAS/dmp/enc

Letters of Apology

November 20, 2006

Mr. Arthur Bear Chief
c/o Department of Justice, Canada
211 Bank of Montreal Building
10199-101 Street
Edmonton, AB T5J 3Y4

Dear Mr. Bear Chief,

I am writing to you on behalf of the Anglican Church of
Canada to offer sincere apologies for the pain and suffering
you experienced during your years at the Old Sun Indian
Residential School.

The Anglican Church of Canada was involved in running
a number of Indian Residential Schools, from their earliest
beginnings up until 1969. Although there was never any intention to cause harm or suffering to the children who attended
these schools, we do acknowledge that there were a few staff
who took advantage of children by physically and sexually
abusing them. Such behaviour was wrong and can never
be excused. We do not now, and never did, condone this
behaviour. The Anglican Church of Canada is deeply sorry
that your school years, which should have been filled with fun
and learning, were instead filled with fear and dread.

It is my hope that the hurt caused by your experiences at the Old Sun Residential School will eventually heal, and that you will find peace, fulfillment and enjoyment in your future.

Yours sincerely,

Archdeacon Michael Pollesel
General Secretary

GOVERNMENT OF CANADA
"Statement of Reconciliation"
Jane Stewart,
Minister of Indian Affairs and Northern Development
January 7, 1998

As Aboriginal and non-Aboriginal Canadians seek to move forward together in a process of renewal, it is essential that we deal with the legacies of the past affecting the Aboriginal peoples of Canada, including the First Nations, Inuit, and Métis. Our purpose is not to rewrite history but, rather, to learn from our past and to find ways to deal with the negative impacts that certain historical decisions continue to have in our society today.

The ancestors of First Nations, Inuit, and Métis peoples lived on this continent long before explorers from other continents first came to North America. For thousands of years before this country was founded, they enjoyed their own forms of government. Diverse, vibrant Aboriginal nations had ways of life rooted in fundamental values concerning their relationships to the Creator, the environment, and each other, in the role of Elders as the living memory of their ancestors, and in their responsibilities as custodians of the lands, waters and resources of their homelands.

The assistance and spiritual values of the Aboriginal peoples who welcomed the newcomers to this continent too often have been forgotten. The contributions made by all Aboriginal peoples to Canada's development, and the contributions that they continue to make to our society today, have not been properly acknowledged. The Government of Canada today, on behalf of all Canadians, acknowledges these contributions.

Sadly, our history with respect to the treatment of Aboriginal people is not something in which we can take pride. Attitudes of racial and cultural superiority led to a suppression of Aboriginal culture and values. As a country, we are burdened by past actions that resulted in weakening the identity of Aboriginal peoples, suppressing their languages and cultures, and outlawing spiritual practices. We must recognize the impact of these actions on the once self-sustaining nations that were disaggregated, disrupted, limited or even destroyed by the dispossession of traditional territory, by the relocation of Aboriginal people, and by some provisions of the Indian Act. We must acknowledge that the result of these actions was the erosion of the political, economic and social systems of Aboriginal people and nations.

Against the backdrop of these historical legacies, it is a remarkable tribute to the strength and endurance of Aboriginal people that they have maintained their historic diversity and identity. The Government of Canada today formally expresses to all Aboriginal people in Canada our profound regret for past actions of the federal government which have contributed to these difficult pages in the history of our relationship together.

One aspect of our relationship with Aboriginal people over this period that requires particular attention is the Residential School system. This system separated many children from their families and communities and prevented them from speaking their own languages and from learning about their heritage and cultures. In the worst cases, it left legacies of personal pain and distress that continue to reverberate in Aboriginal communities to this day. Tragically, some children were victims of physical and sexual abuse.

The Government of Canada acknowledges the role it played in the development and administration of these schools. Particularly to those individuals who experienced the tragedy of sexual and physical abuse at residential schools, and who have carried this burden believing that in some way they must be responsible, we wish to emphasize that what you experienced was not your fault and should never have happened. To those of you who suffered this tragedy at residential schools, we are deeply sorry.

In dealing with the legacies of the Residential School system, the Government of Canada proposes to work with First Nations, Inuit, and Métis people, the Churches and other interested parties to resolve the longstanding issues that must be addressed. We need to work together on a healing strategy to assist individuals and communities in dealing with the consequences of this sad era of our history.

No attempt at reconciliation with Aboriginal people can be complete without reference to the sad events culminating in the death of Métis leader Louis Riel. These events cannot be undone; however, we can and will continue to look for ways of affirming the contributions of Métis people in Canada and of reflecting Louis Riel's proper place in Canada's history.

Reconciliation is an ongoing process. In renewing our partnership, we must ensure that the mistakes which marked our past relationship are not repeated. The Government of Canada recognizes that policies that sought to assimilate Aboriginal people, women and men, were not the way to build a strong country. We must instead continue to find ways in which Aboriginal people can participate fully in the economic, political, cultural and social life of Canada in a manner which preserves and enhances the collective identities of Aboriginal communities, and allows them to evolve and flourish in the future. Working together to achieve our shared goals will benefit all Canadians, Aboriginal and non-Aboriginal alike.

March 26, 2007

PROTECTED A

Mr. Arthur Bear Chief

Dear Mr. Bear Chief:

I write today in light of the settlement you reached with the Government of Canada as a result of the abuse you suffered at the Old Sun Indian Residential School. The Government accepts its responsibility for what happened to you at the school.

On behalf of the Minister responsible for Indian Residential Schools Resolution Canada, The Honourable Jim Prentice, and the Government of Canada, I wish to apologize to you and your family and to express the Government's sincere and deep regret for all of the pain that you and your family have suffered as a result of your attendance at Old Sun. I recognize that you have carried this burden with you for many years. I wish to emphasize that what you experienced was not your fault and should never have happened.

You have shown considerable courage and dignity in coming forward to talk about extremely personal and painful experiences. I hope that by recounting these very painful experiences, you have a measure of comfort which will allow you and your family to move forward with your lives.

Sincerely,

Peter Harrison

For Further Reading

Archibald, Jo-ann. *Indigenous Storywork: Educating the Heart, Mind, Body, and Spirit.* Vancouver: University of British Columbia Press, 2008.

Arthur H. *The Grieving Indian.* Winnipeg: Intertribal Christian Communications, 1988.

Bastien, Betty. *Blackfoot Ways of Knowing: The Worldview of the Siksikaitsitapi.* Calgary: University of Calgary Press, 2004.

Bombay, Amy, Kim Matheson, and Hymie Anisman. "Intergenerational Trauma: Convergence of Multiple Processes Among First Nations Peoples in Canada." *Journal of Aboriginal Health* 5, no. 3 (November 2009): 6–47.

Chief Dan George. *My Heart Soars*. Saanichton, BC: Hancock House, 1974.

Corntassel, Jeff, Chaw-win-is, and T'lakwadzi. "Indigenous Storytelling, Truth-Telling and Community Approaches to Reconciliation." *English Studies in Canada* 35, no. 1 (March 2009): 137–59.

Dion, Susan D. *Braiding Histories: Learning from Aboriginal Peoples' Experiences and Perspectives*. Vancouver: University of British Columbia Press, 2008.

Mahoney, Kathleen. "The Indian Residential School Settlement: Is Reconciliation Possible?" *ABlawg. ca* (University of Calgary, Faculty of Law), 26 June 2013, http://ablawg.ca/wp-content/uploads/2013/06/Blog_KM_Settlement_June2013.pdf.

McLeod, Neal. "Coming Home Through Stories." *International Journal of Canadian Studies* 18 (Fall 1998): 51–66.

Merasty, Joseph August, with David Carpenter. *The Education of Augie Merasty: A Residential School Memoir*. Regina: University of Regina Press, 2015.

Metatawabin, Edmund, with Alexandra Shimo. *Up Ghost River: A Chief's Journey Through the Turbulent Waters of Native History*. Toronto: Vintage Canada, 2014.

Miller, J. R. "Residential Schools and Reconciliation." *ActiveHistory.ca*, 19 February 2013. http://activehistory.ca/papers/history-papers-13/.

————. *Shingwauk's Vision: A History of Native Residential Schools*. Toronto: University of Toronto Press, 1996.

Million, Dian. "Telling Secrets: Sex, Power and Narratives in Indian Residential School Histories." *Canadian Woman Studies* 20, no. 2 (2000): 92–104.

Milloy, John S. *A National Crime: The Canadian Government and the Residential School System 1879 to 1986*. Winnipeg: University of Manitoba Press, 1999.

Niezen, Ronald. *Truth and Indignation: Canada's Truth and Reconciliation Commission on Indian Residential Schools*. Toronto: University of Toronto Press, 2013.

Regan, Paulette. *Unsettling the Settler Within: Indian Residential Schools, Truth Telling, and Reconciliation in Canada*. Vancouver: University of British Columbia Press, 2011.

Rogers, Shelagh, Mike DeGagné, and Jonathan Dewar, eds. *"Speaking My Truth": Reflections on Reconciliation and Residential School*. Ottawa: Aboriginal Healing Foundation, 2012.

Royal Commission on Aboriginal Peoples. "Residential Schools." In *Report of the Royal Commission on Aboriginal Peoples*, vol. 1, *Looking Forward, Looking Back*, chap. 10. Ottawa: Canada Communication Group, 1996. https://qspace.library.queensu.ca/handle/1974/6874.

Sellars, Bev. *They Called Me Number One: Secrets and Survival at an Indian Residential School.* Vancouver: Talonbooks, 2013.

Stanton, Kim. "Canada's Truth and Reconciliation Commission: Settling the Past?" *International Indigenous Policy Journal* 2, no. 3 (August 2011): article 2. http://ir.lib.uwo.ca/cgi/viewcontent. cgi?article=1034&context=iipj.

Truth and Reconciliation Commission of Canada. *They Came for the Children: Canada, Aboriginal Peoples, and Residential Schools.* Winnipeg: Truth and Reconciliation Commission of Canada, 2012. http://www.myrobust. com/websites/trcinstitution/File/2039_T&R_eng_ web[1].pdf.

———. *Canada's Residential Schools: Final Report of the Truth and Reconciliation Commission of Canada.* 6 vols. Montréal and Kingston: McGill-Queen's University Press, 2015. http://www.trc.ca/websites/trcinstitution/ index.php?p=890.

Wesley-Esquimaux, Cynthia C., and Magdalena Smolewski. *Historic Trauma and Aboriginal Healing.* Ottawa: Aboriginal Healing Foundation, 2004. http:// www.ahf.ca/downloads/historic-trauma.pdf.